Progressive Patterns
Volume 1
Adult Colouring Book

nikk nakk
designs

Progressive Patterns Volume 1 - Adult Colouring Book
Copyright 2015 by nikk nakk designs
Created by Niki Palmer, Ros Tulleners
Illustrated by Stuart Campbell, Subrata Dutta, Elshan Gurbanov

First edition 2015
ISBN: 978-1-925422-01-6
www.nikknakkdesigns.com.au

Welcome to Progressive Patterns Adult Colouring book - a graded collection of 45 your favorite designs from our three Progressive Patterns books - Simple Styles, Decorative Delights and Intricate Inspirations - all in the one place.

Whether you are a raw beginner, an enthusiastic colourist or a dedicated professional, there is a pattern for everyone. Let the book open at any page, pick up your favourite colour and start anywhere.

Colouring has been proven to be a very effective stress reliever - what could be simpler than turning off all your electronic devices, and picking up a coloured pencil.

Lose yourself in the moment as you let the stress of the day drift away and focus completely on releasing your creative spirit as your masterpiece unfold under your fingertips.

Take a chance and use our 'pot luck' method - it is so easy!

- Make a cup of tea or coffee if you need one.
- Find a quiet place to work away from electronic distractions.
- Let the book fall open at any page.
- Close your eyes and pick up any colour.
- Choose a shape and start to colour.
- Woohoo ..... You are a colourist!

It's so easy to unwind as you create your masterpieces with coloured pencils, watercolour pencils, felt tips, gel pens, whatever medium you choose - let your imagination run wild. Each page is unbacked giving you lots of opportunities to experiment with different pens, pencils and tips, using light and heavy pressure for different effects.

There are no rules - just let your creative spirit flow. Before you know it, you will feel calm, renewed and ready to face the world again.

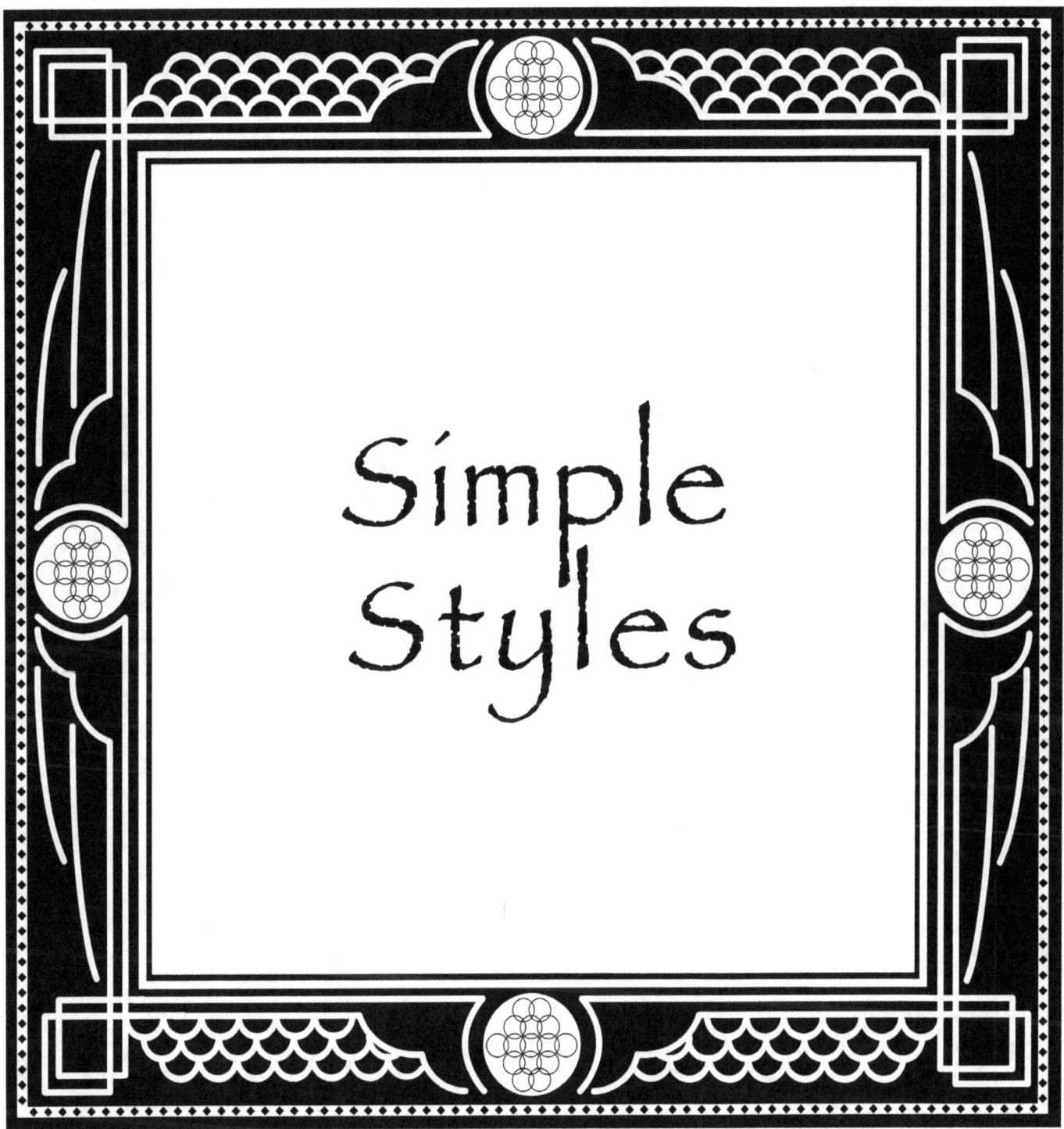

Simple
Styles

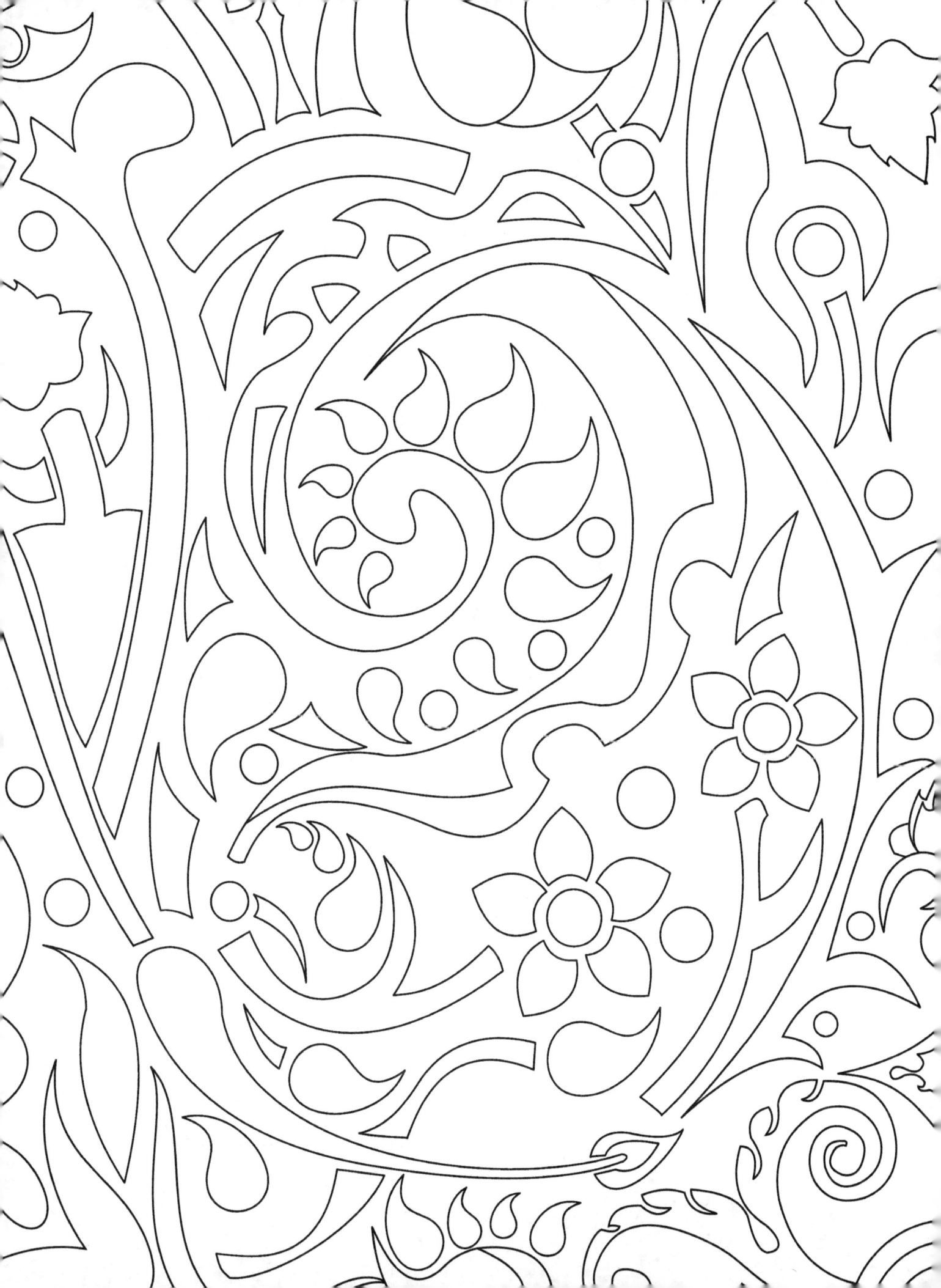

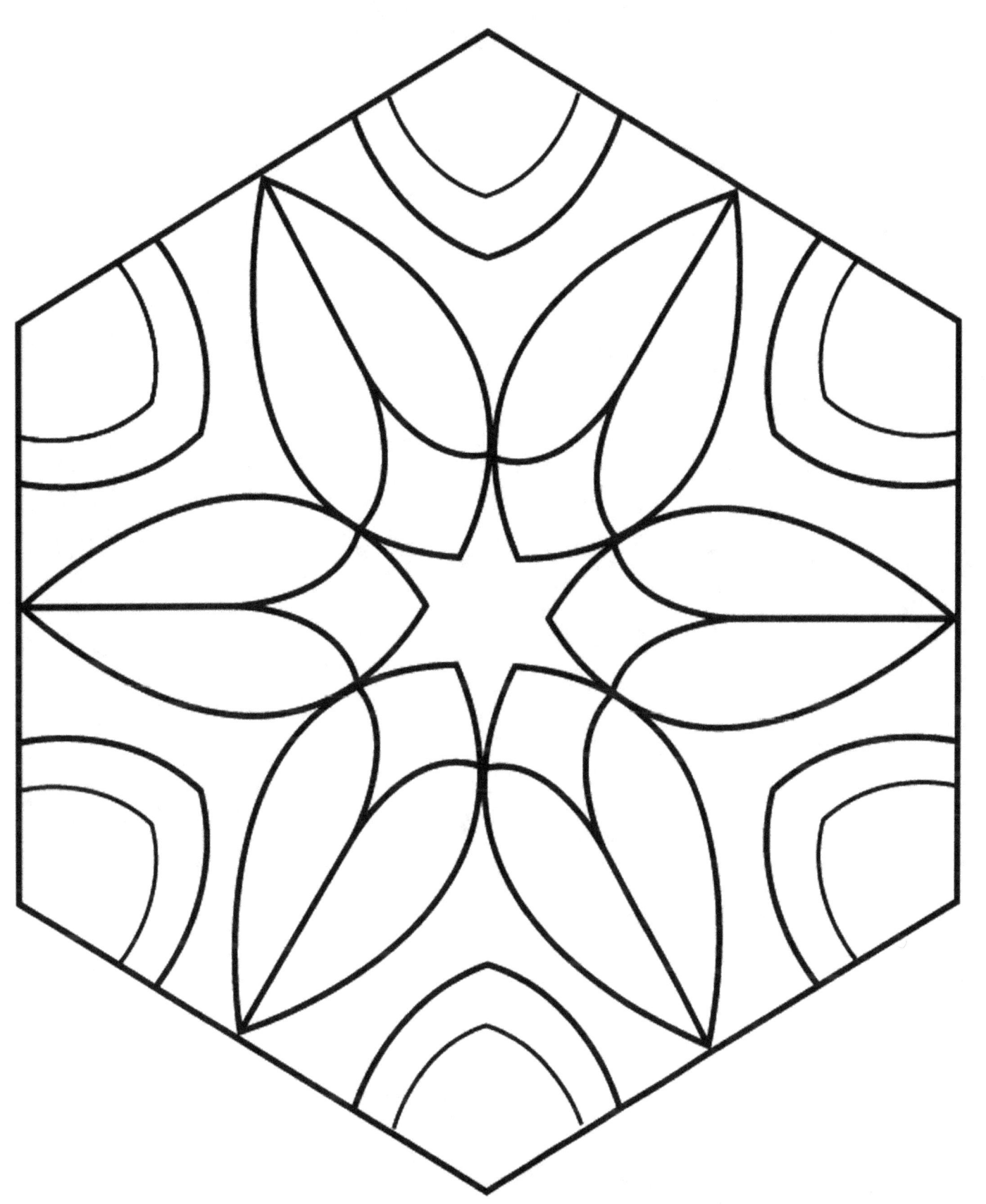

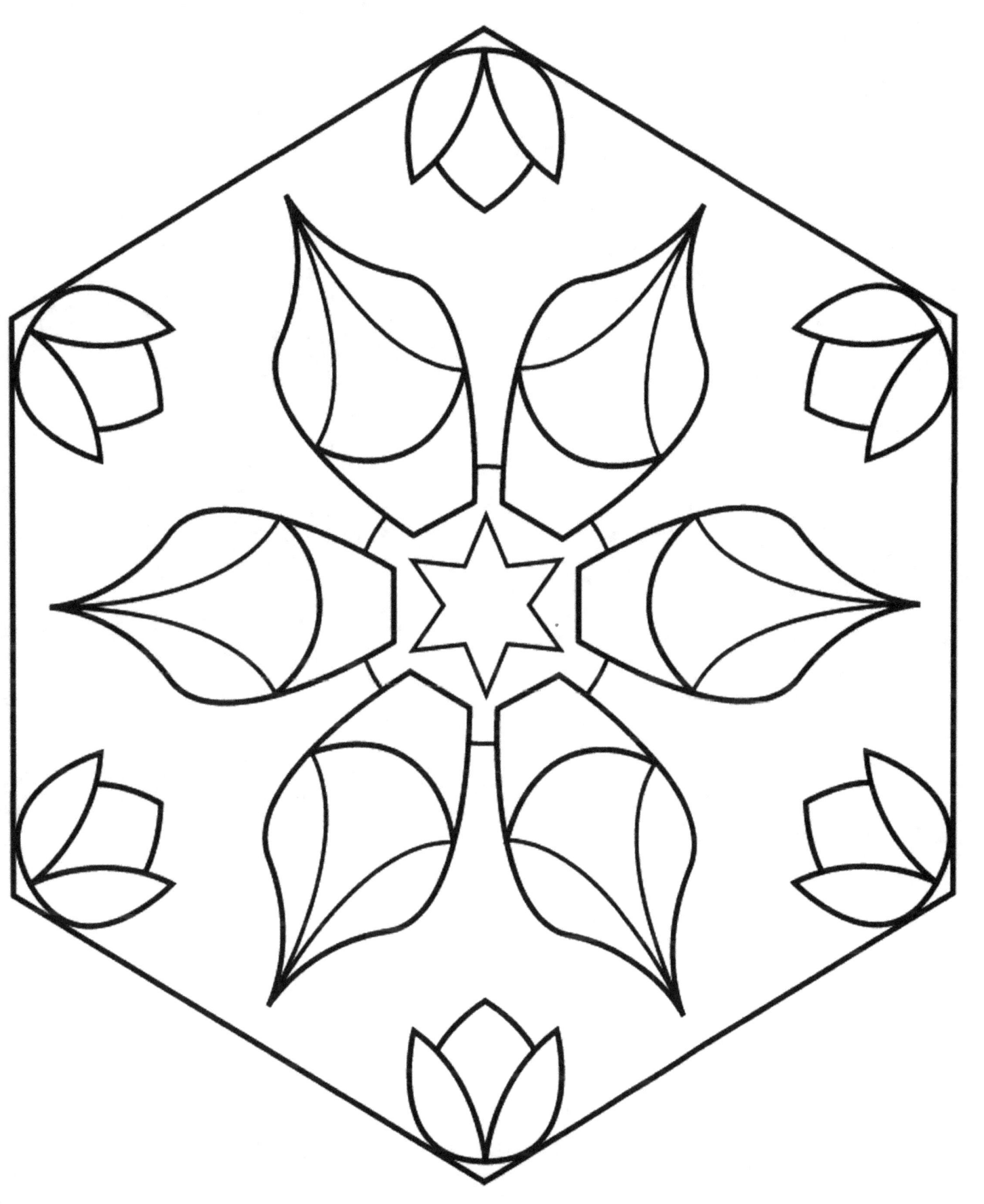

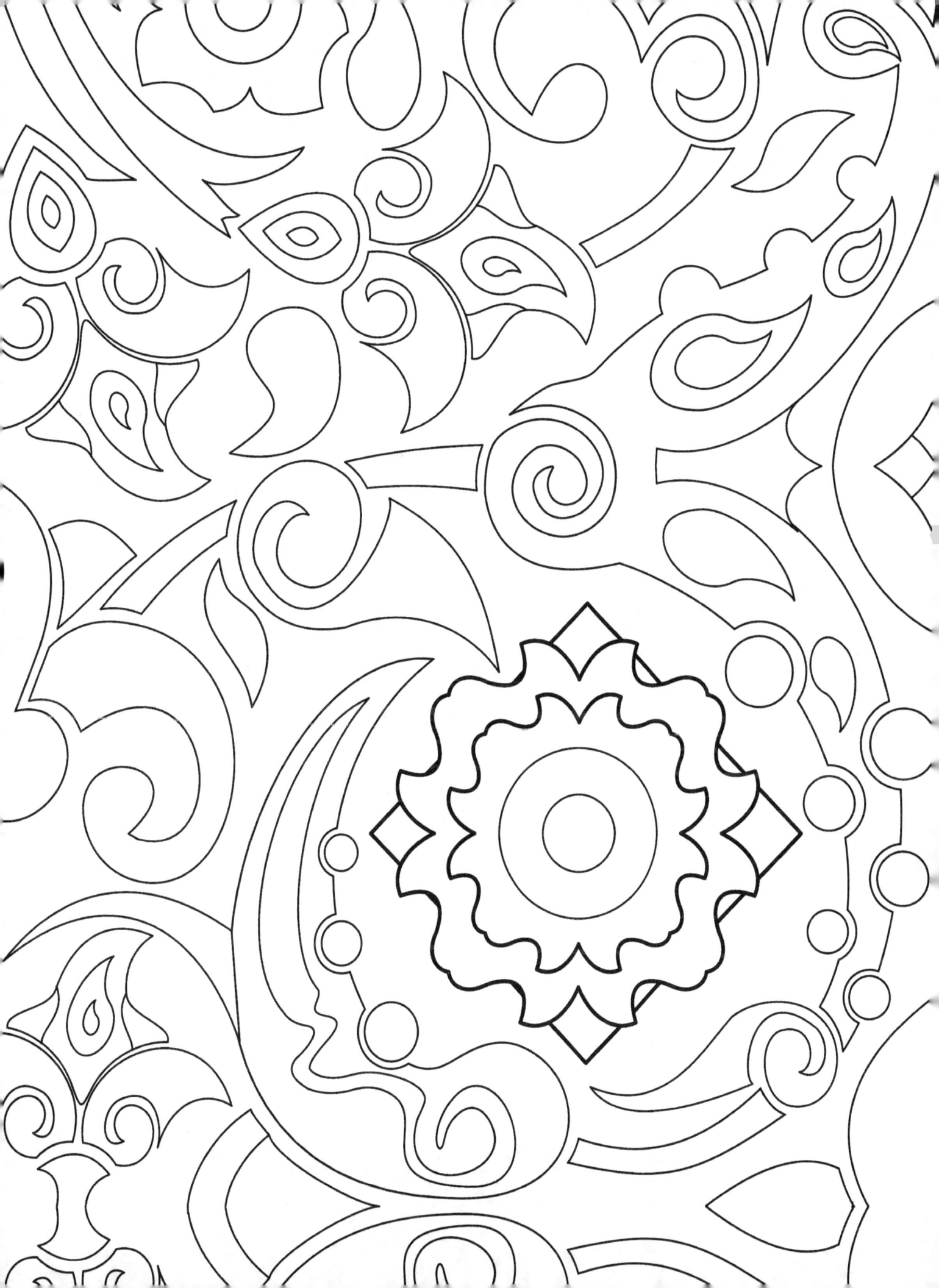

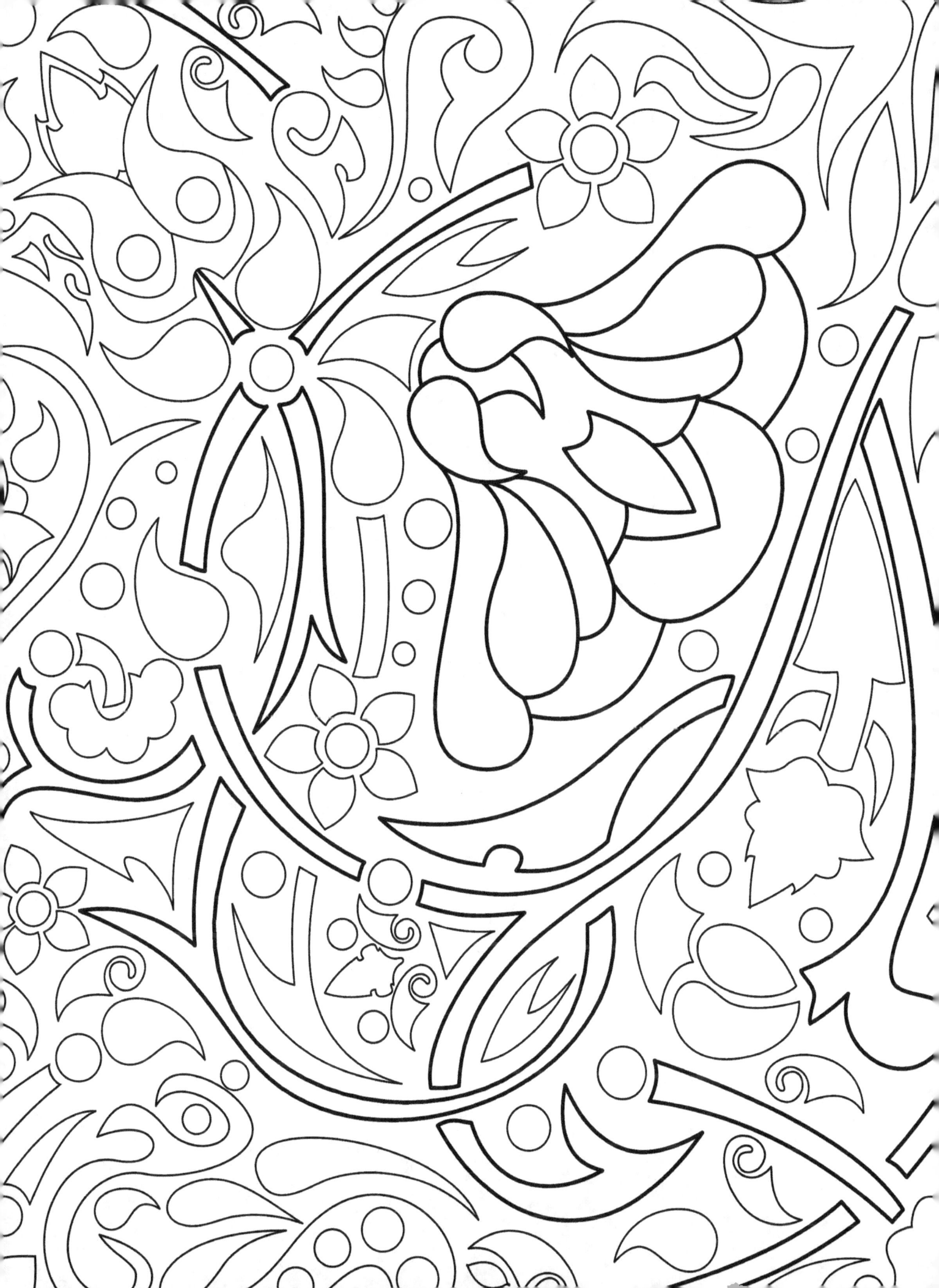

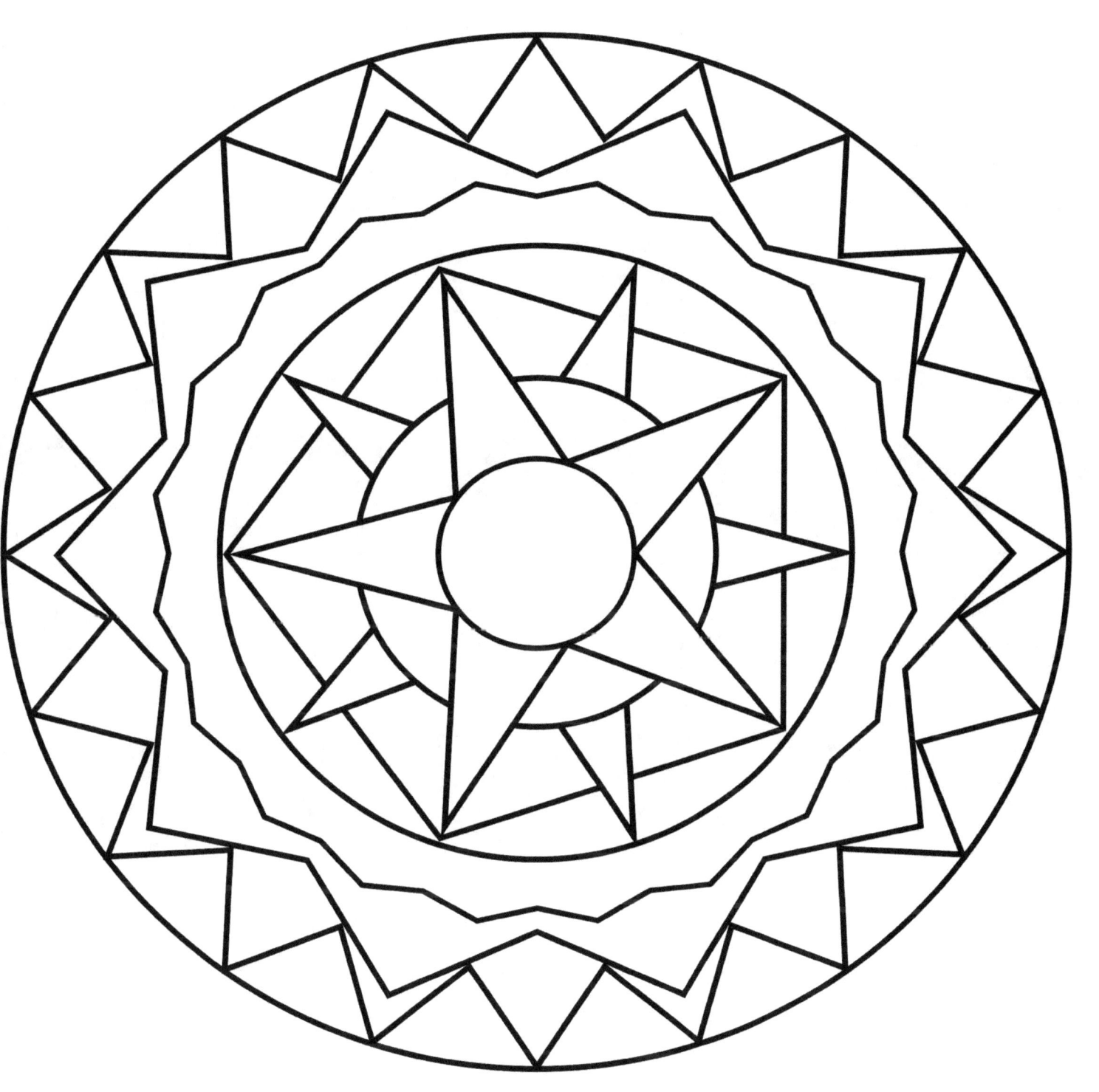

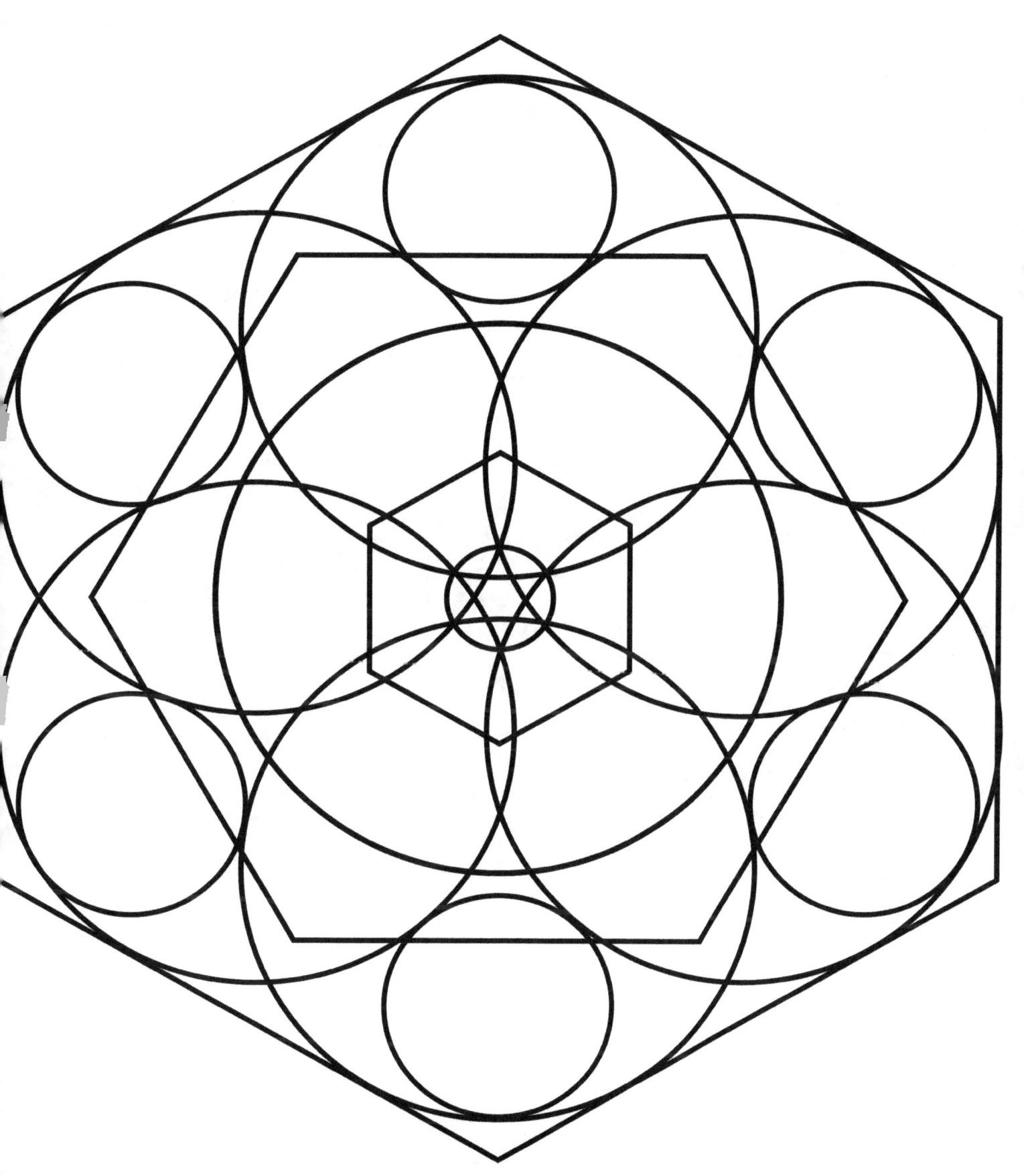

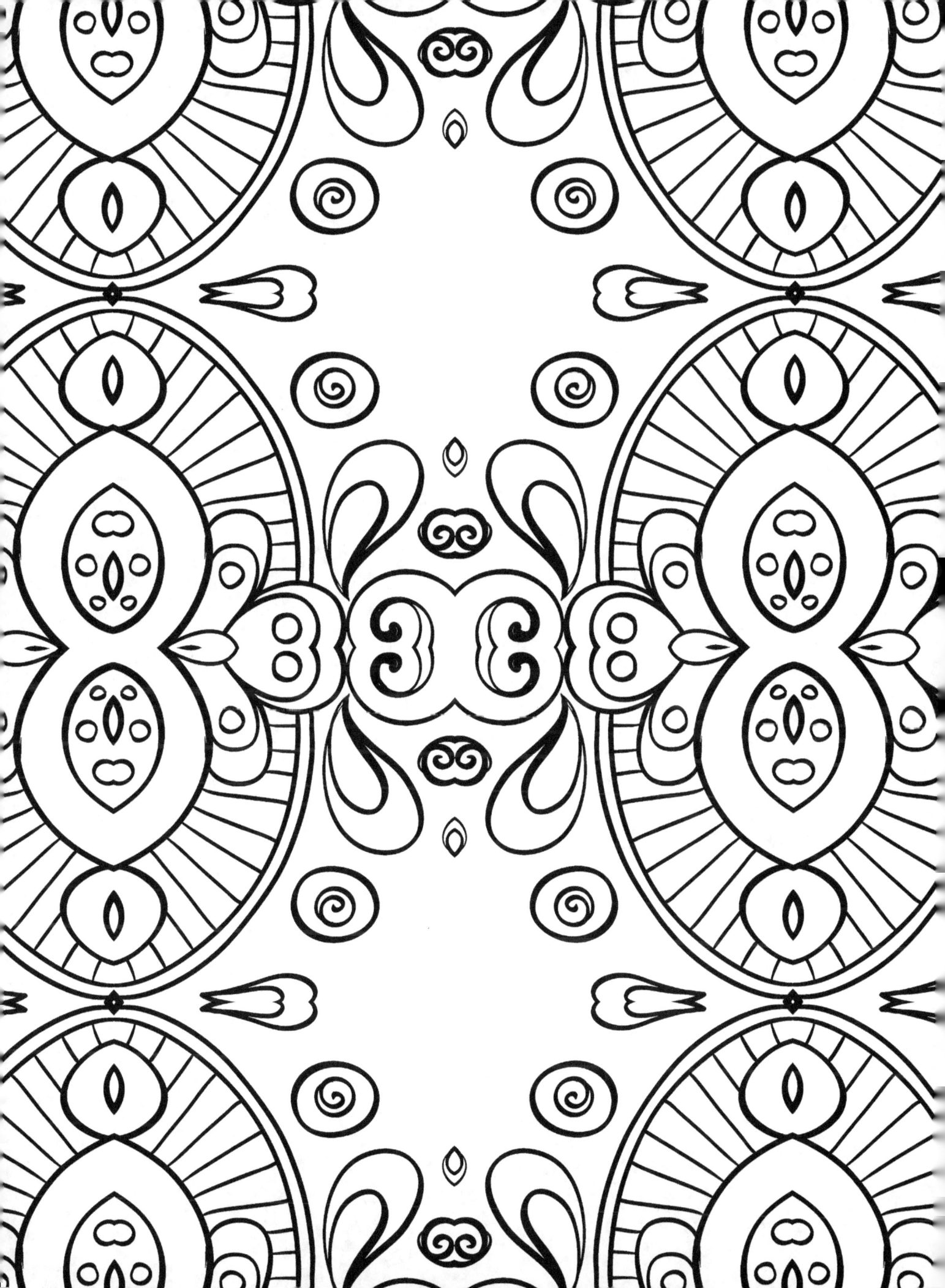

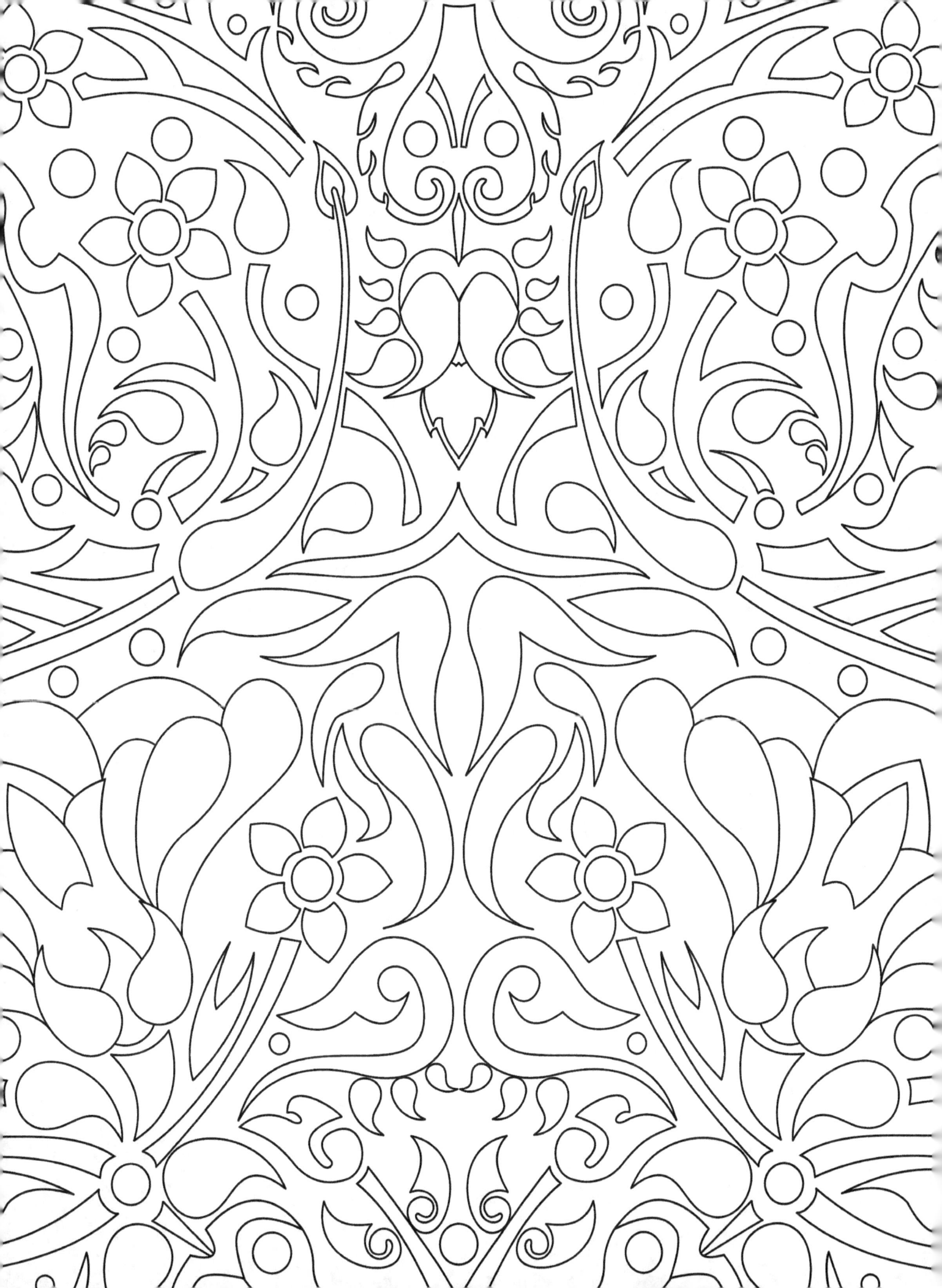

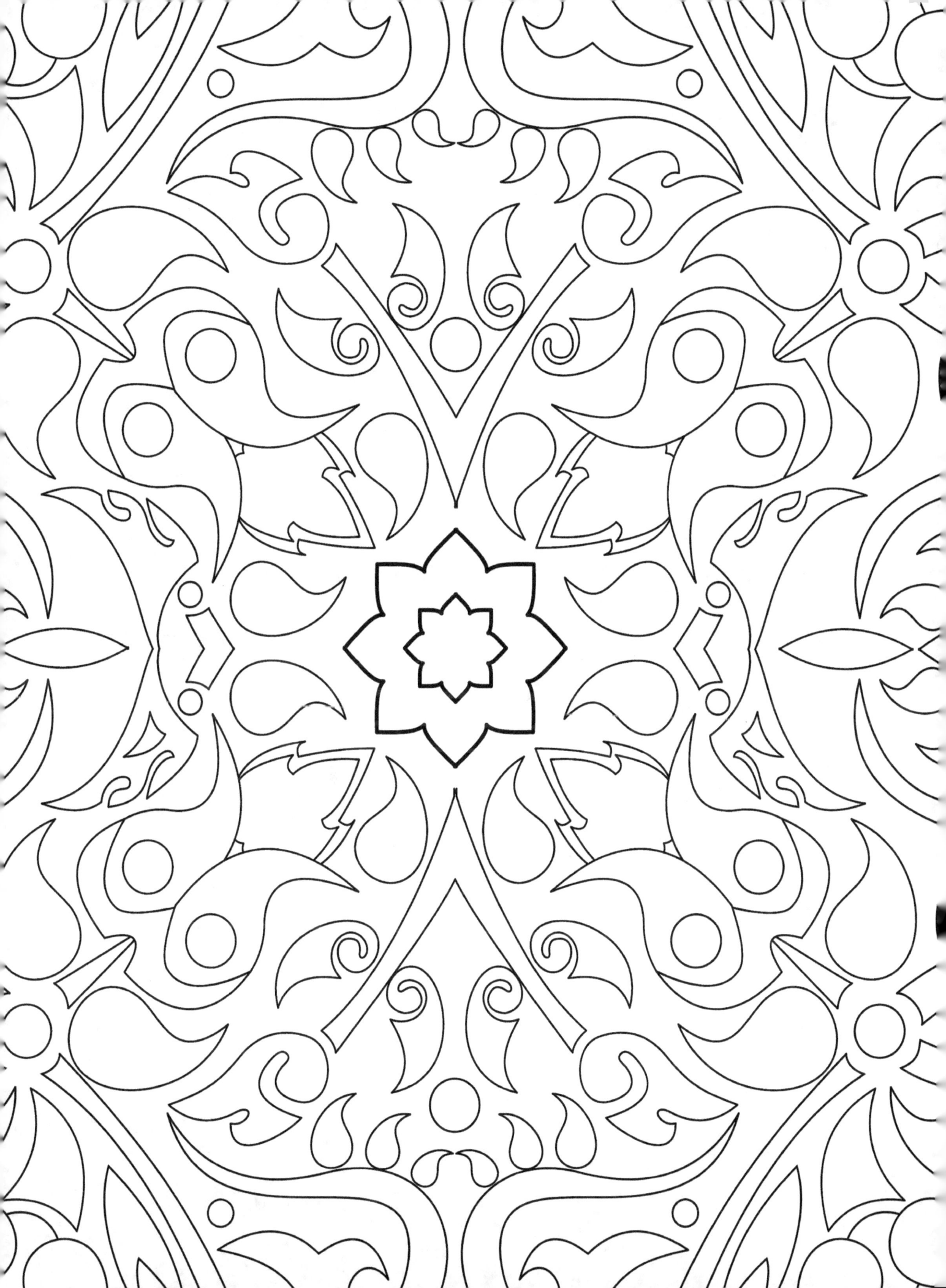

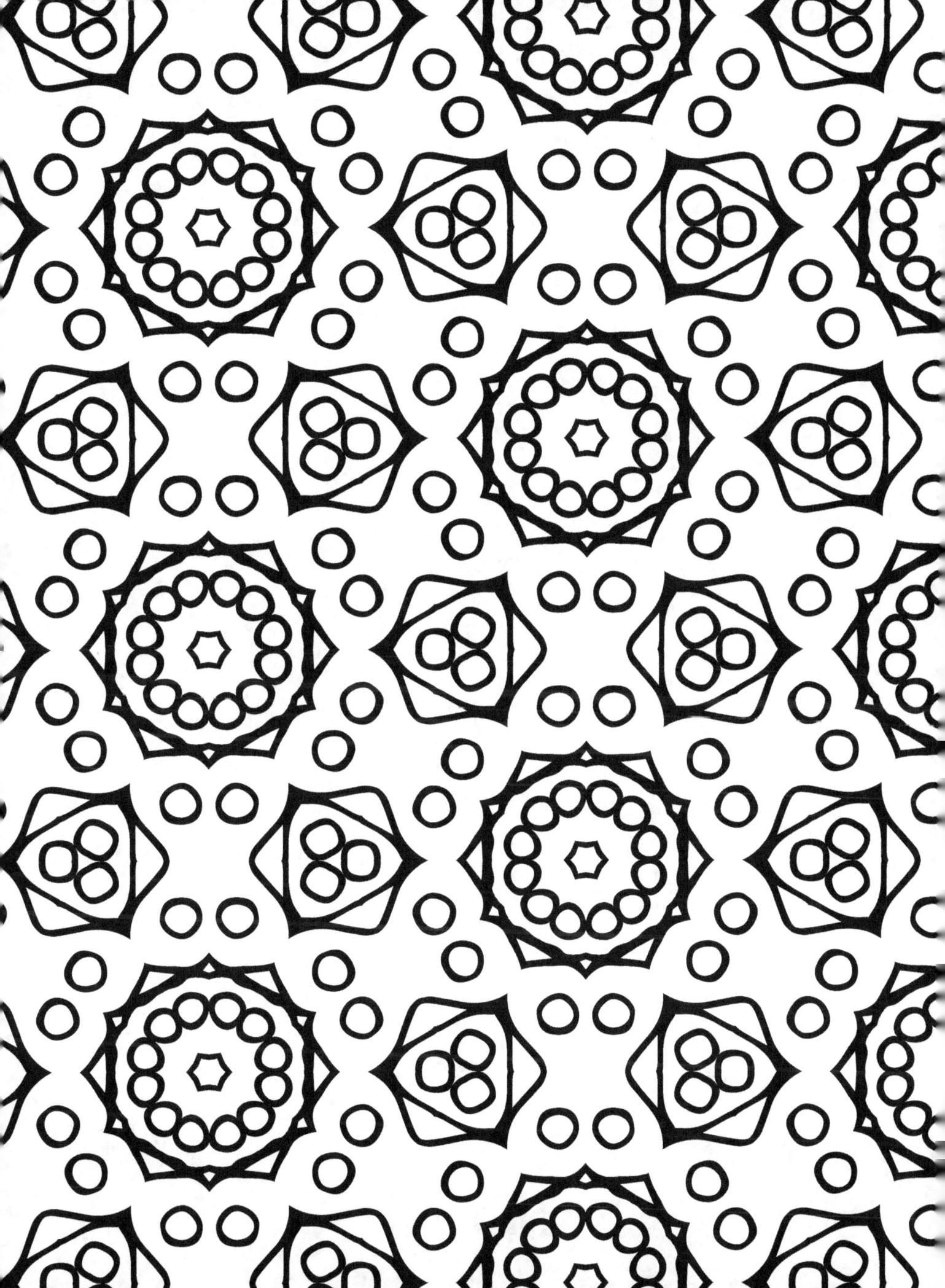

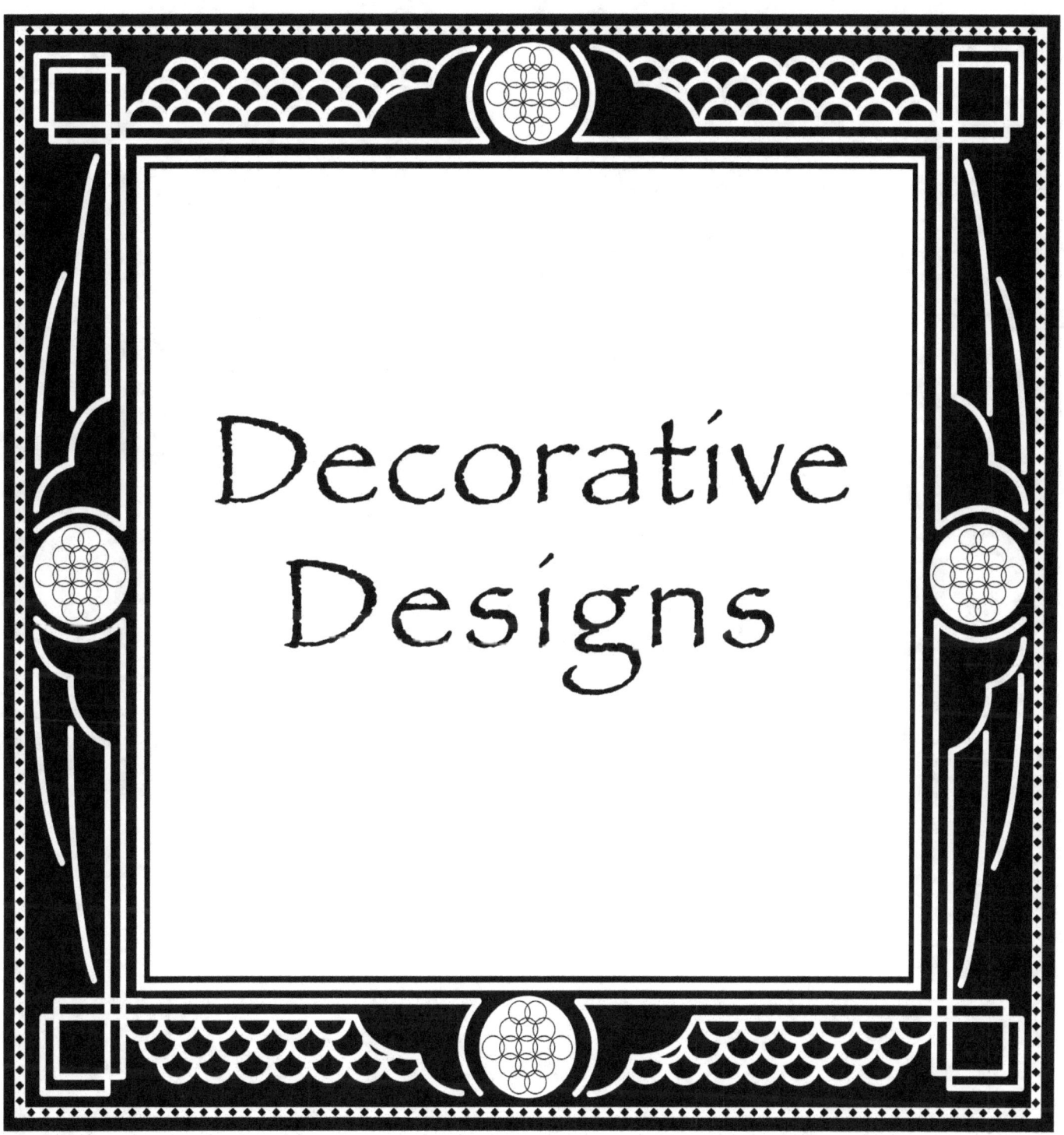

Decorative Designs

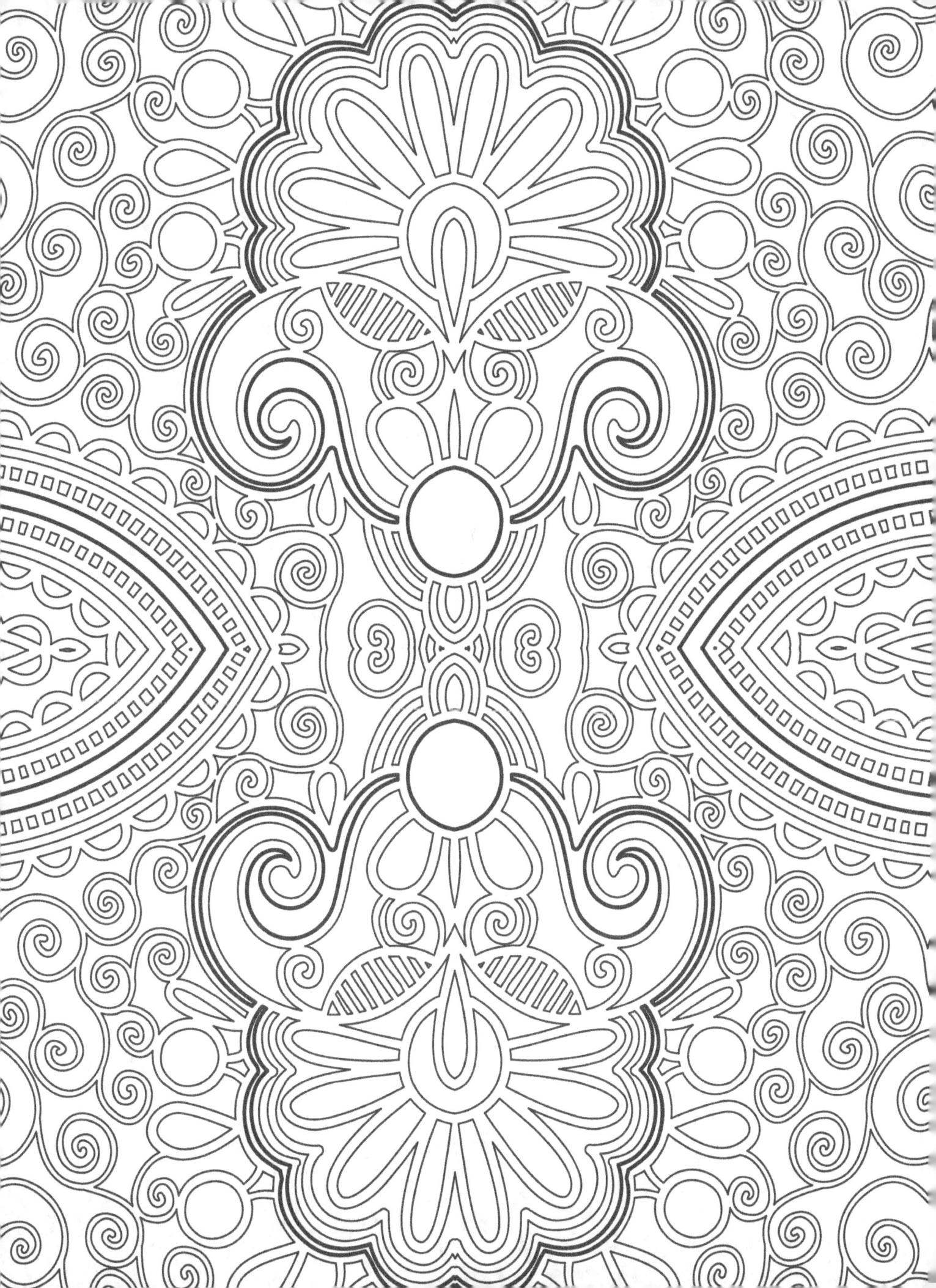

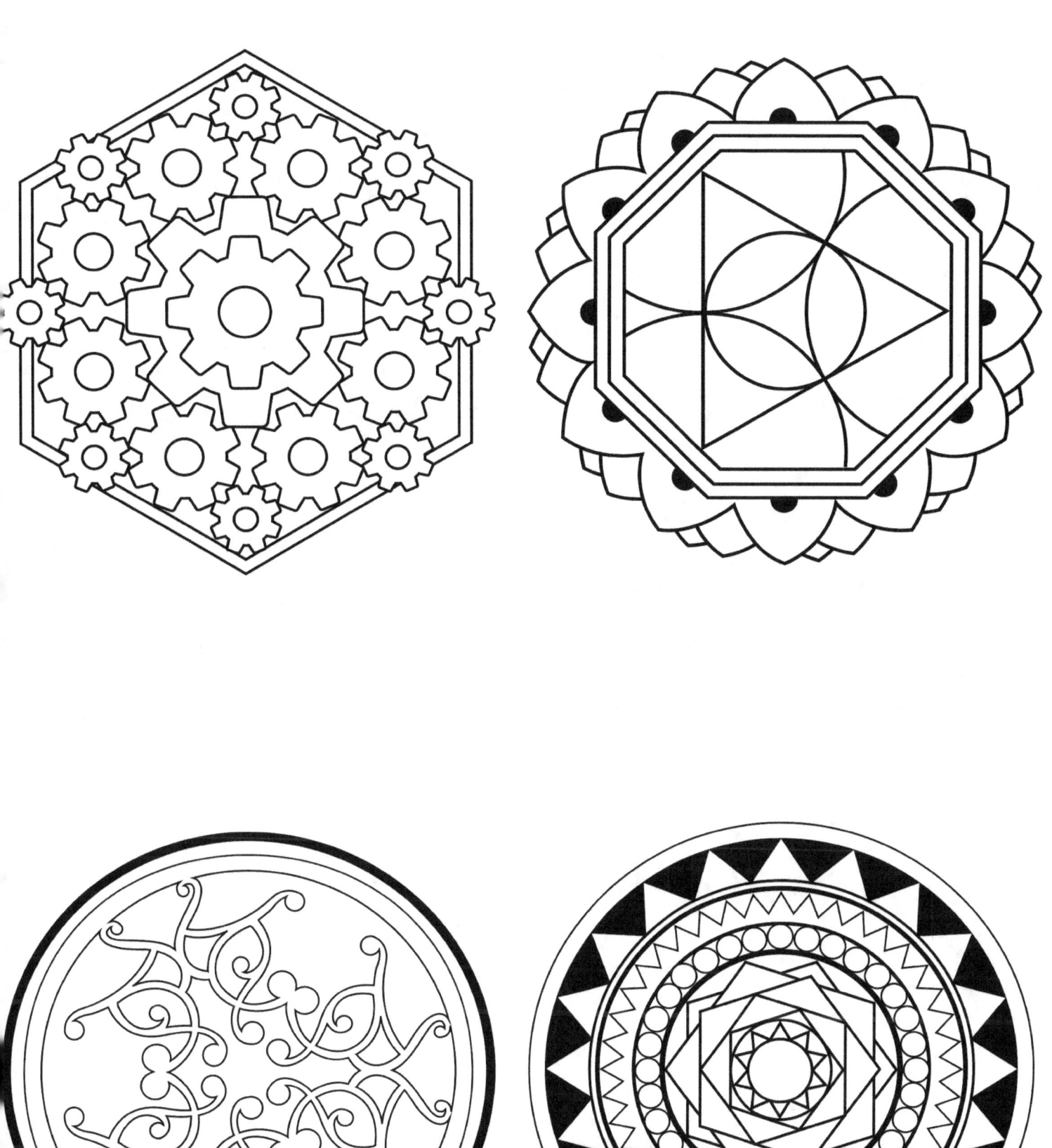

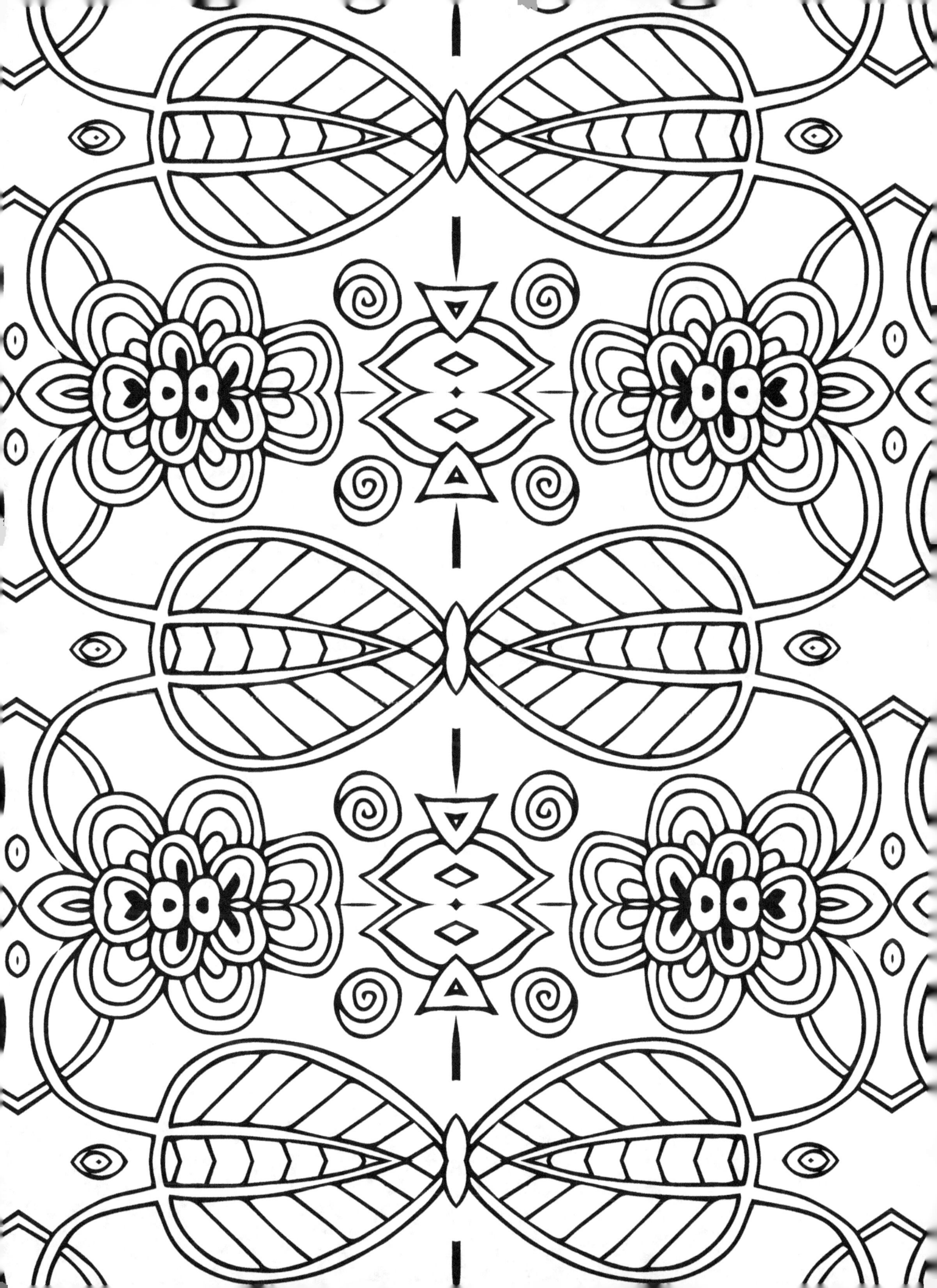

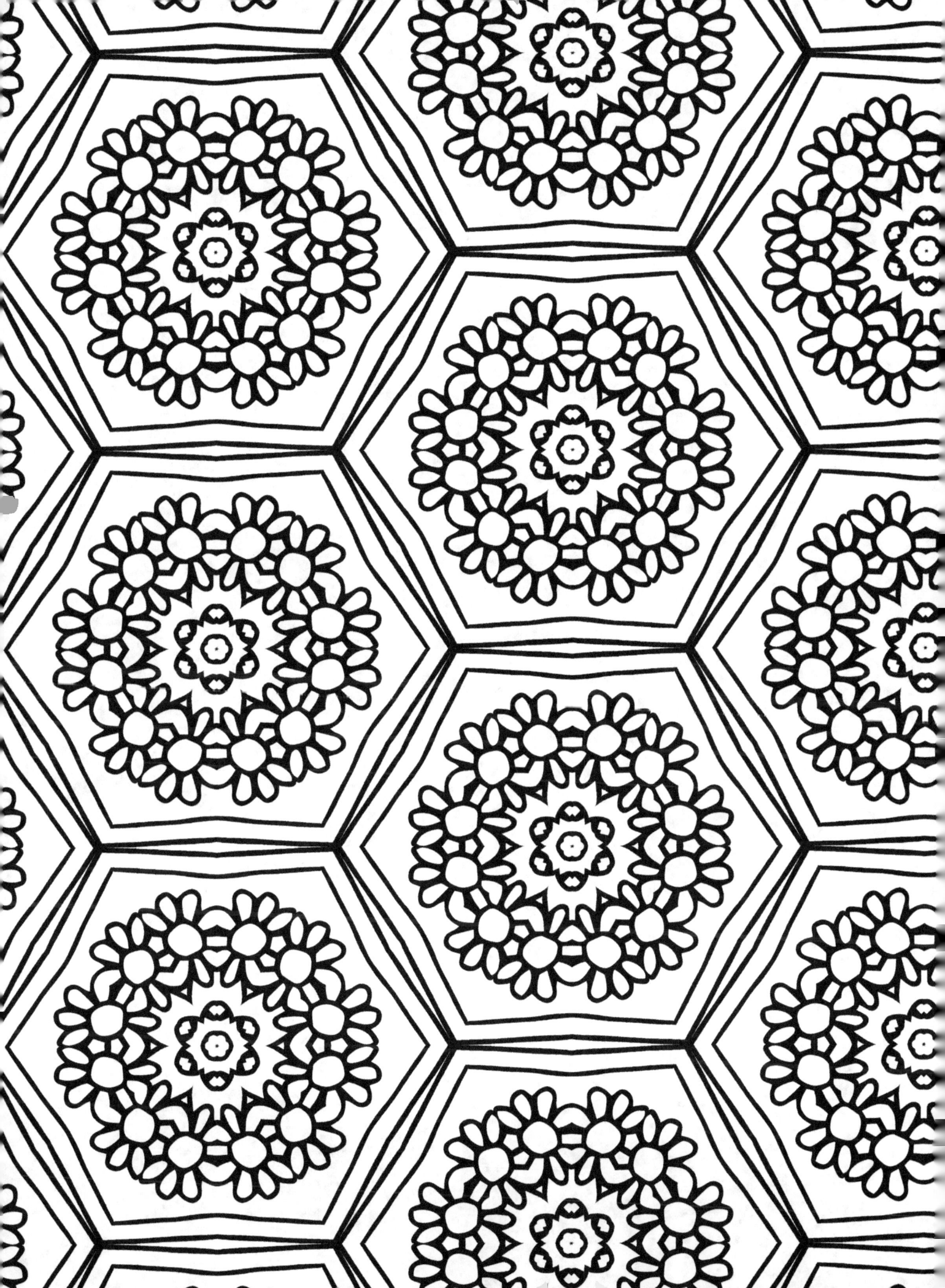

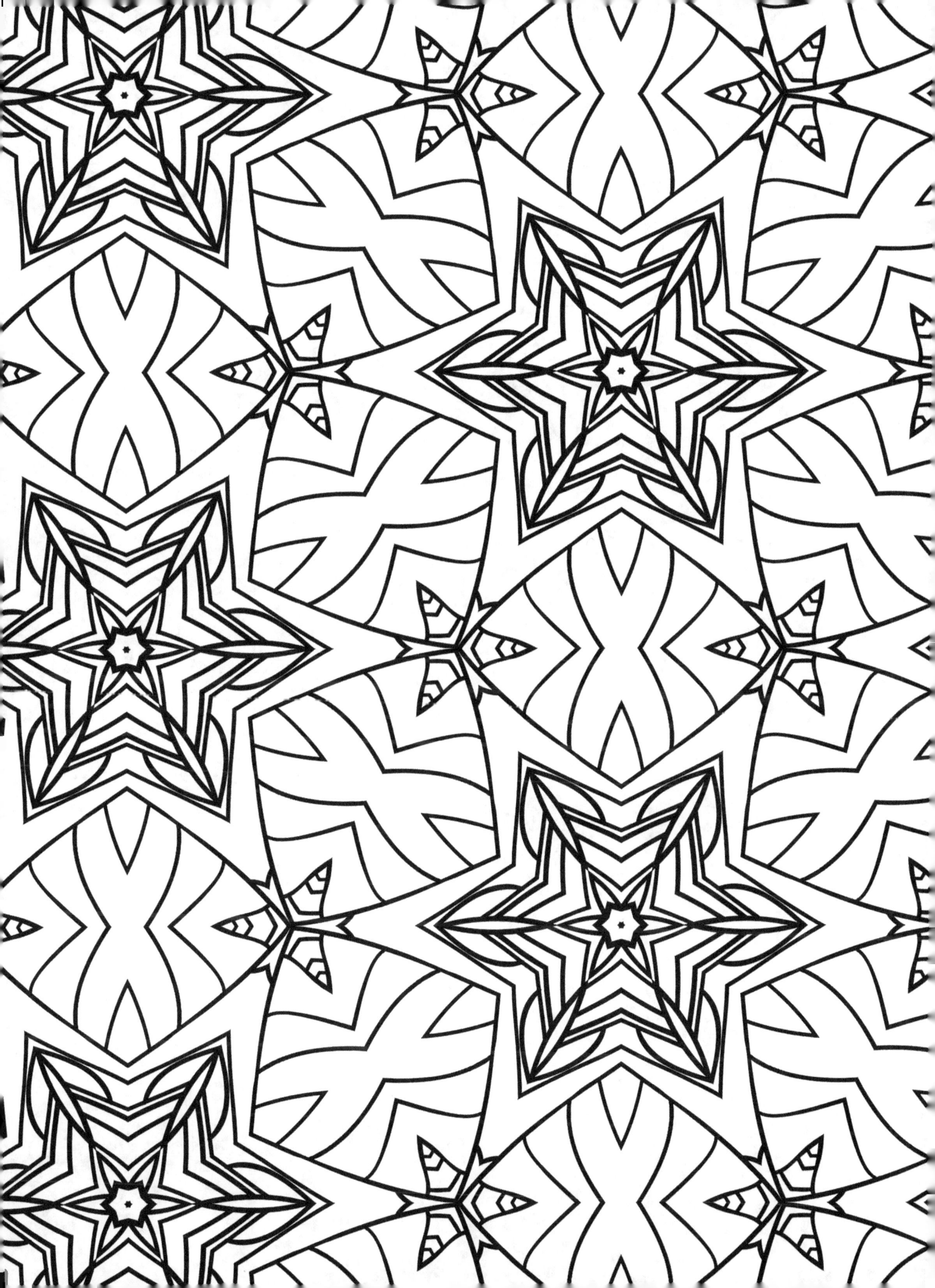

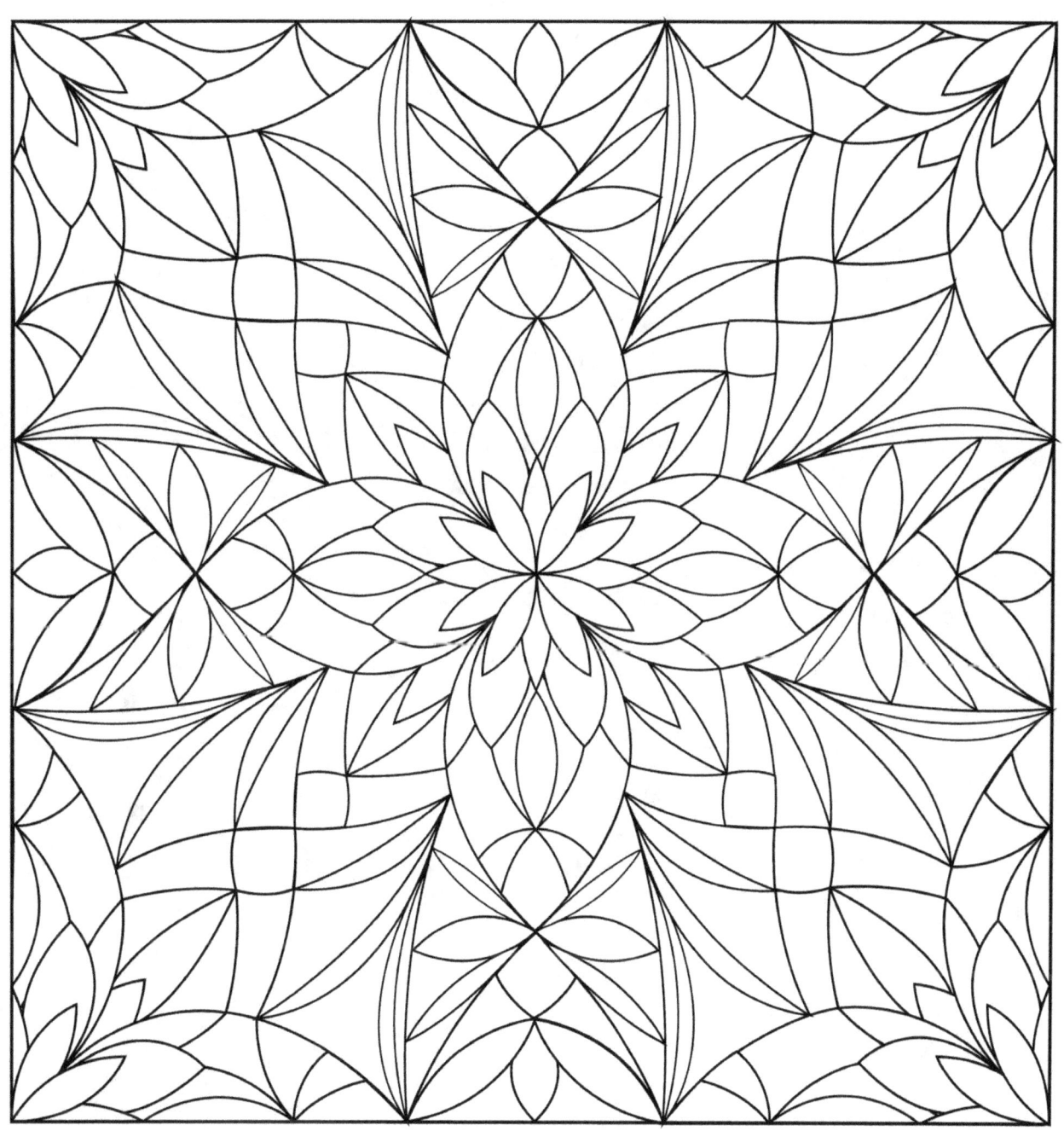

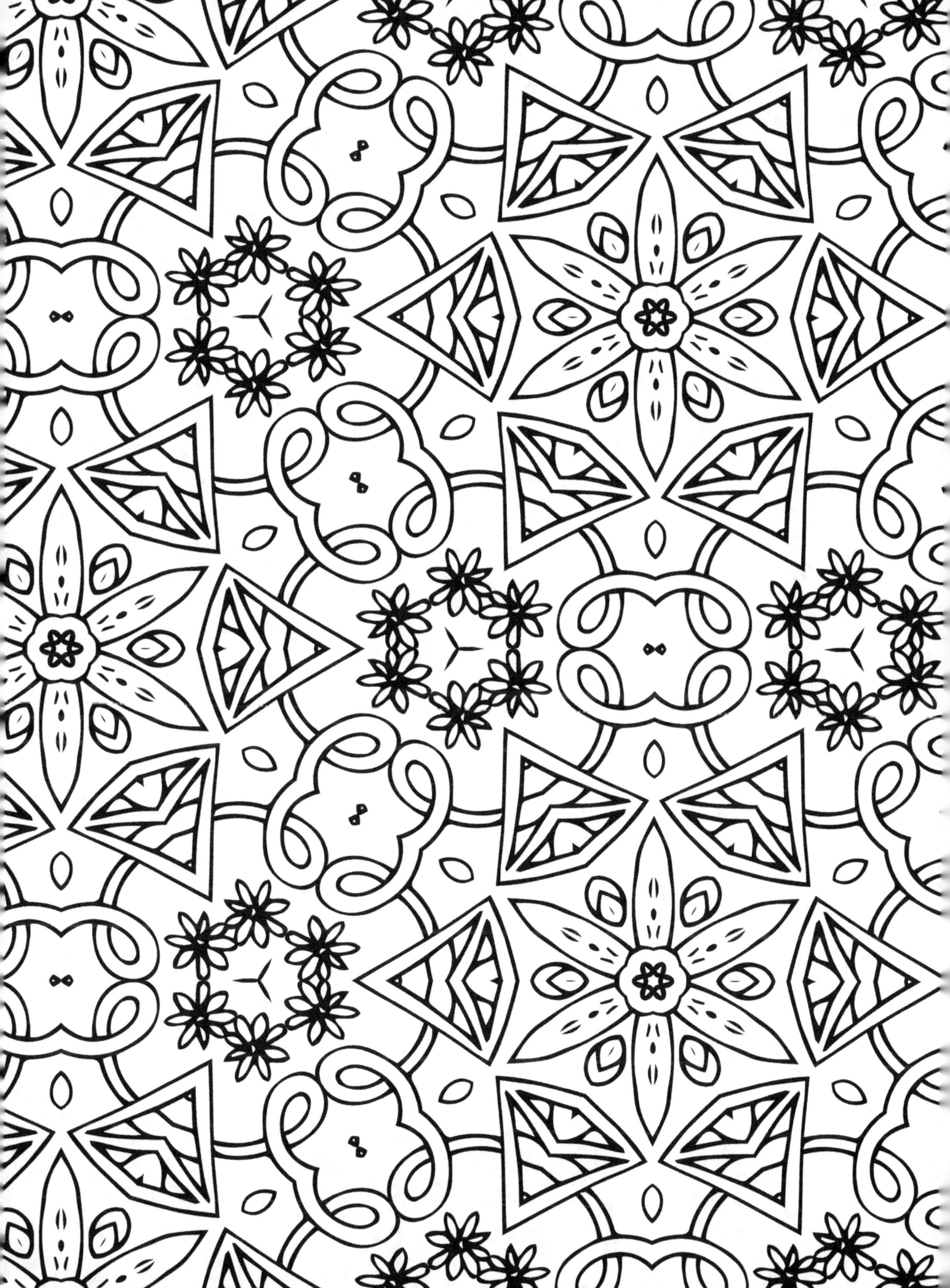

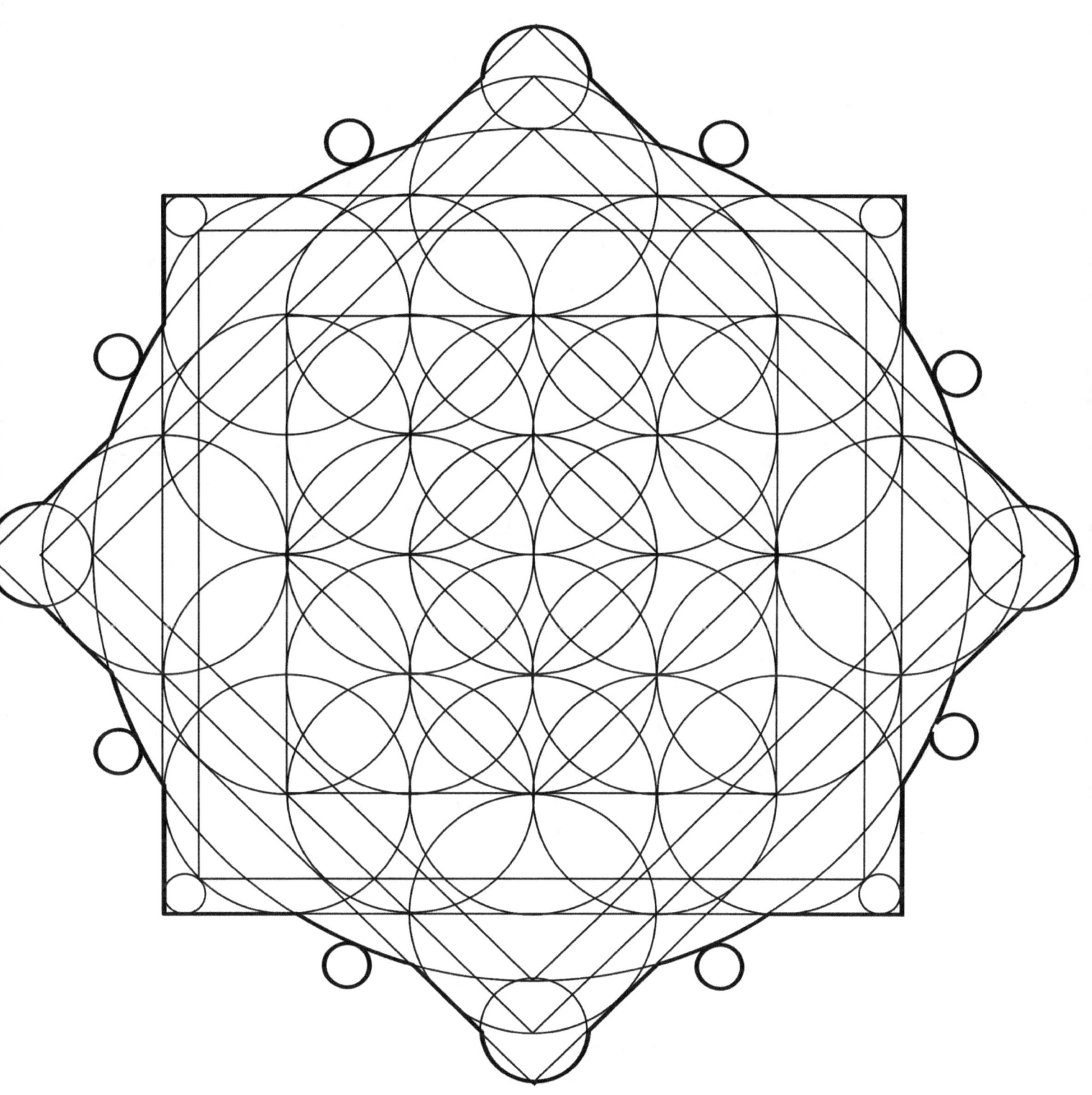

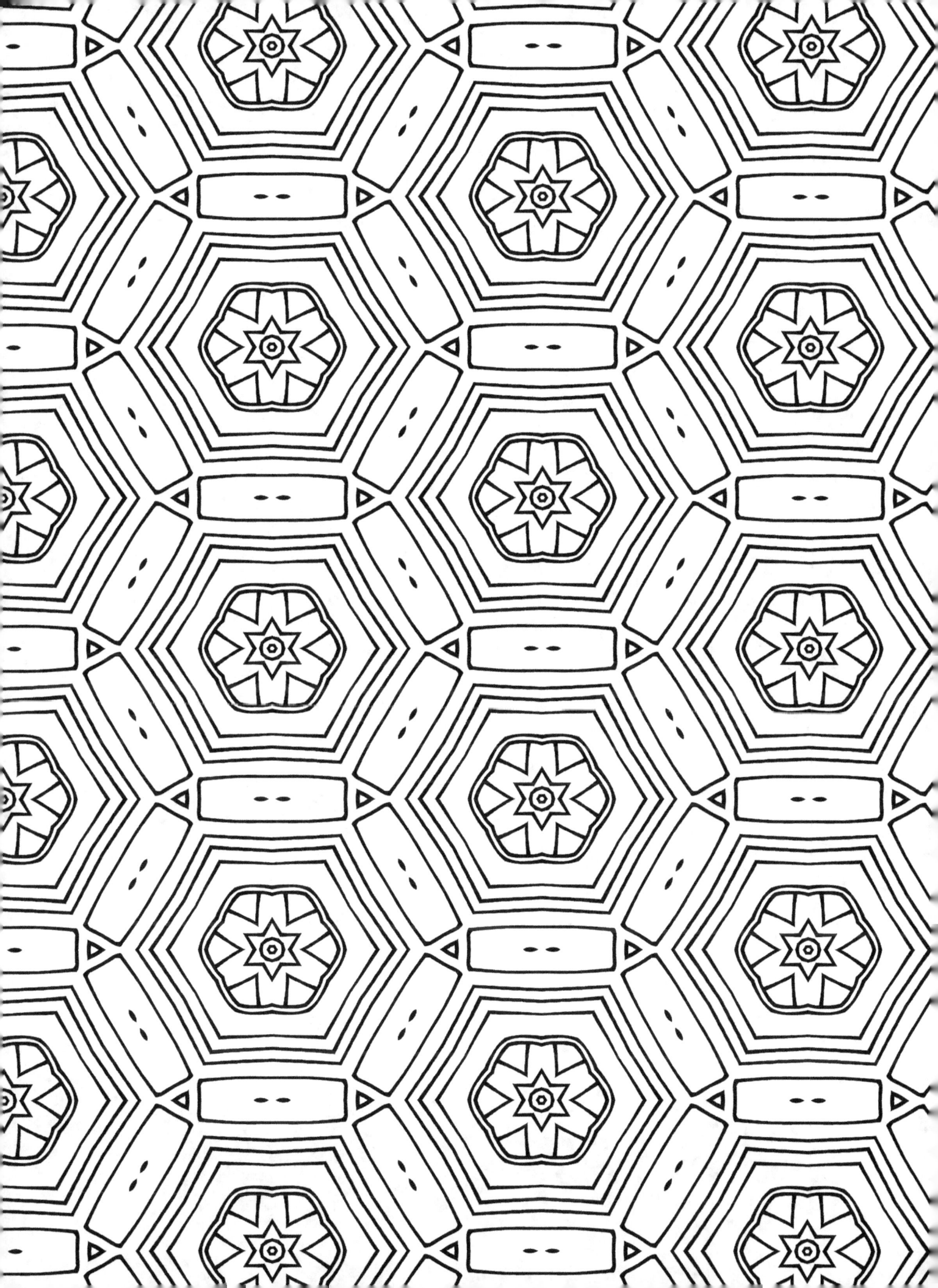

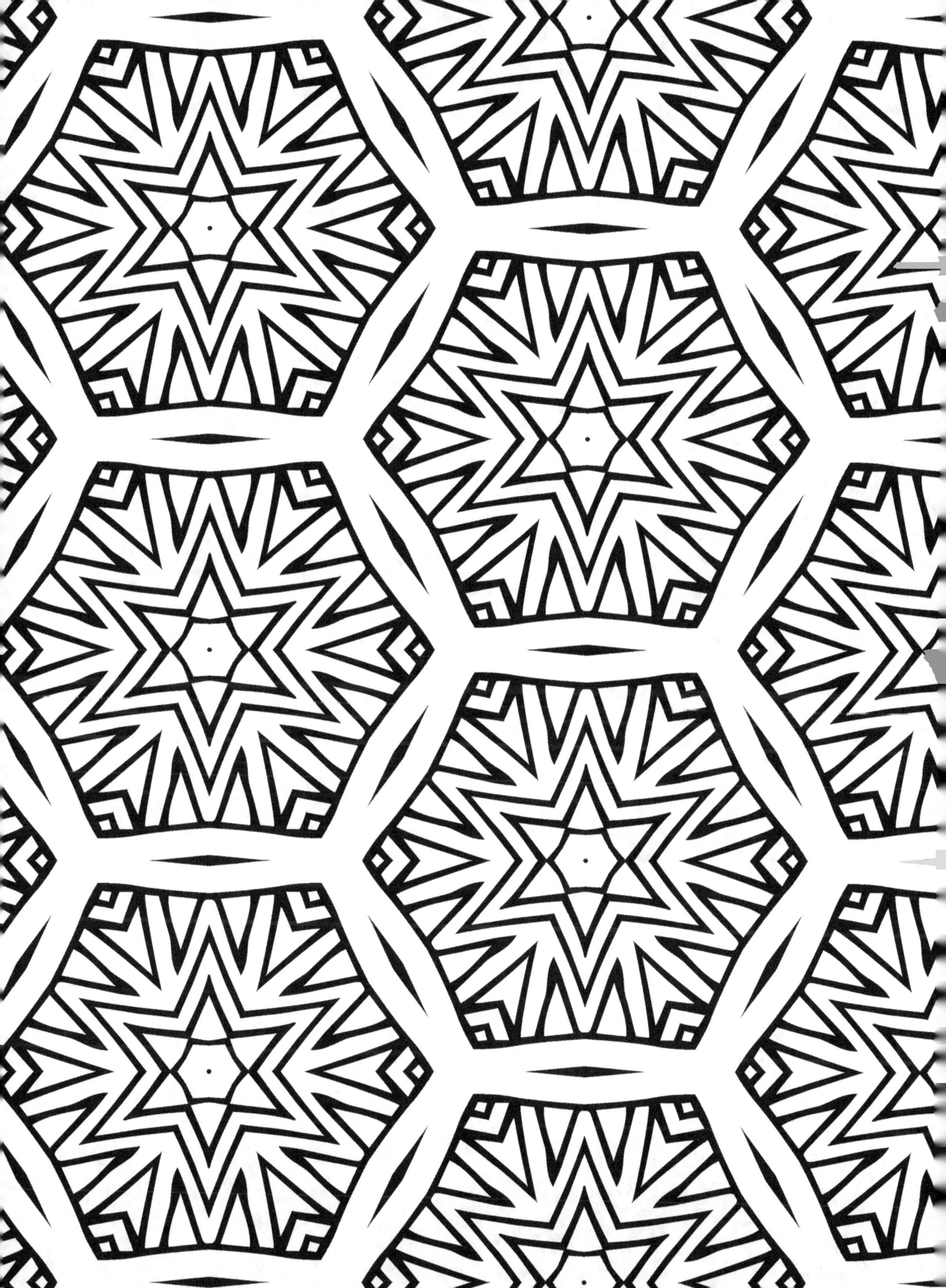

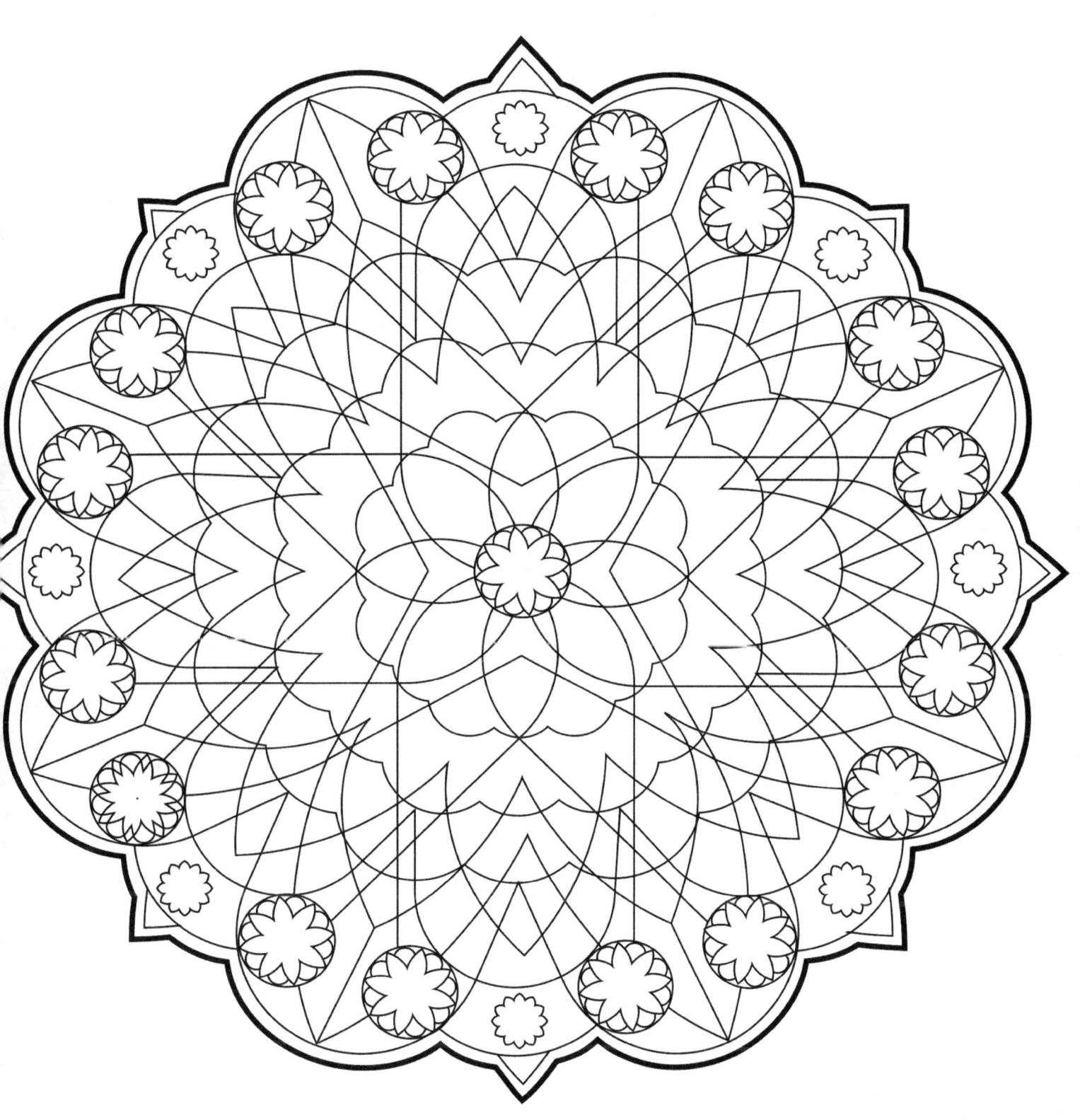

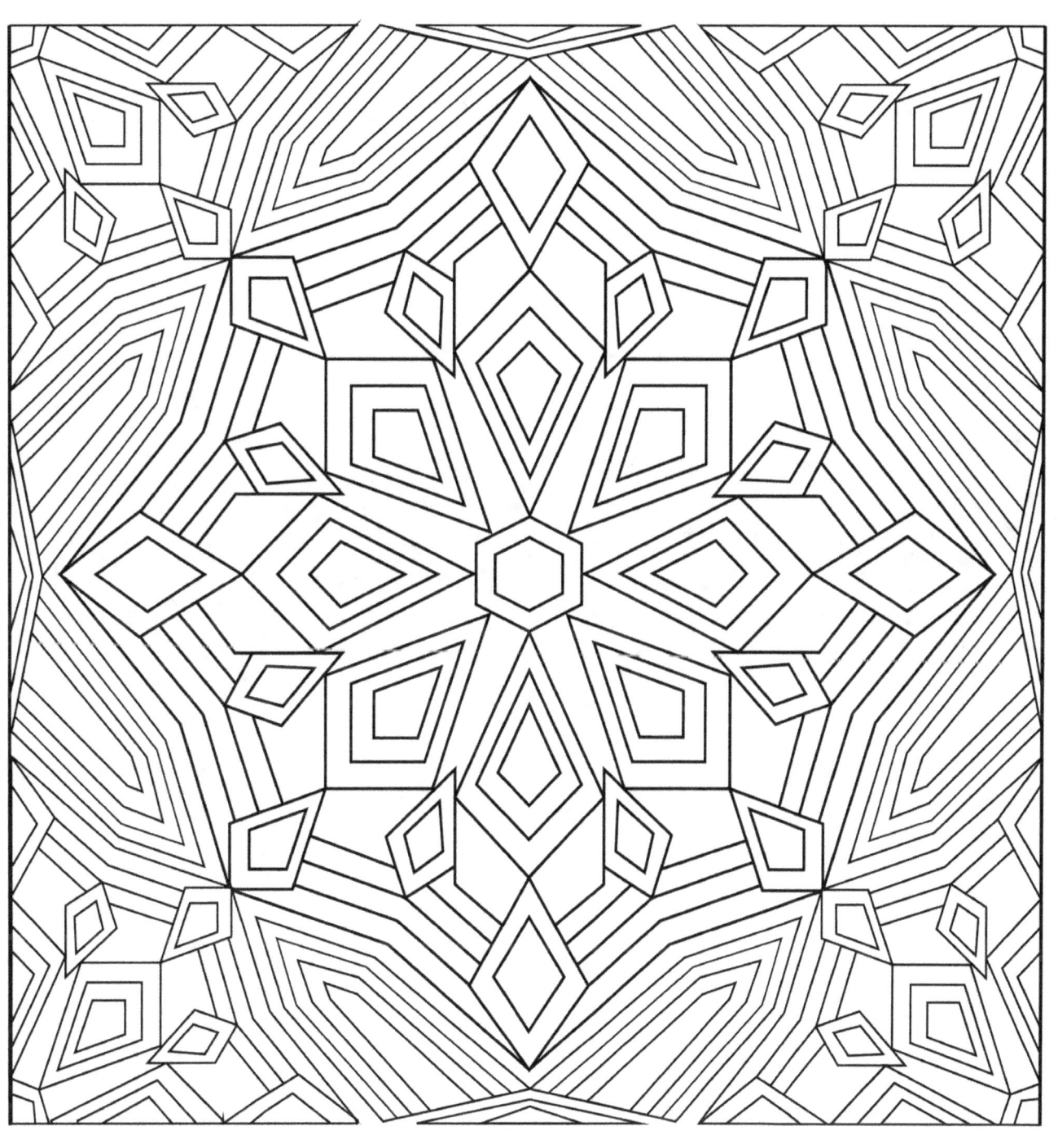

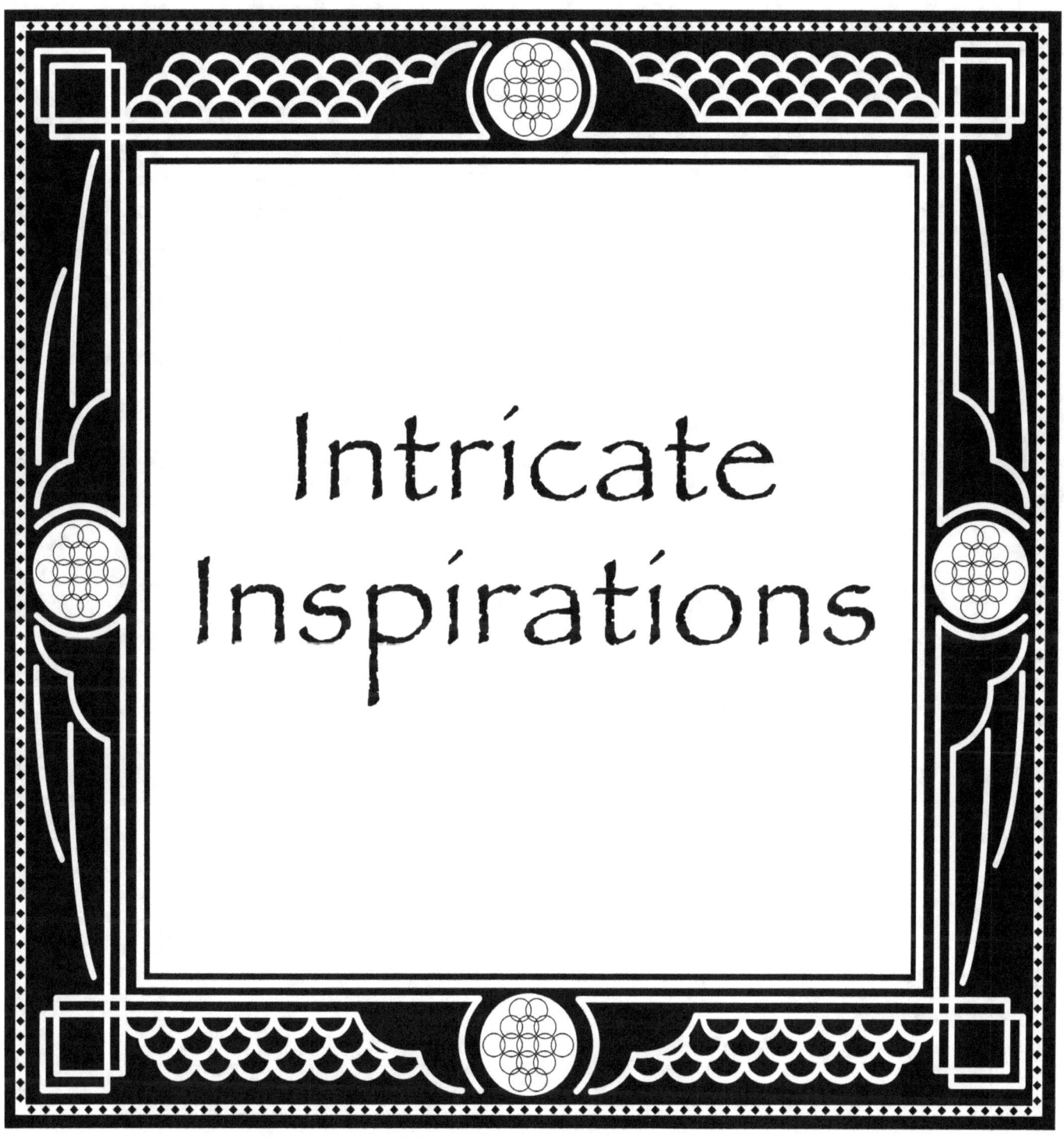

Intricate
Inspirations

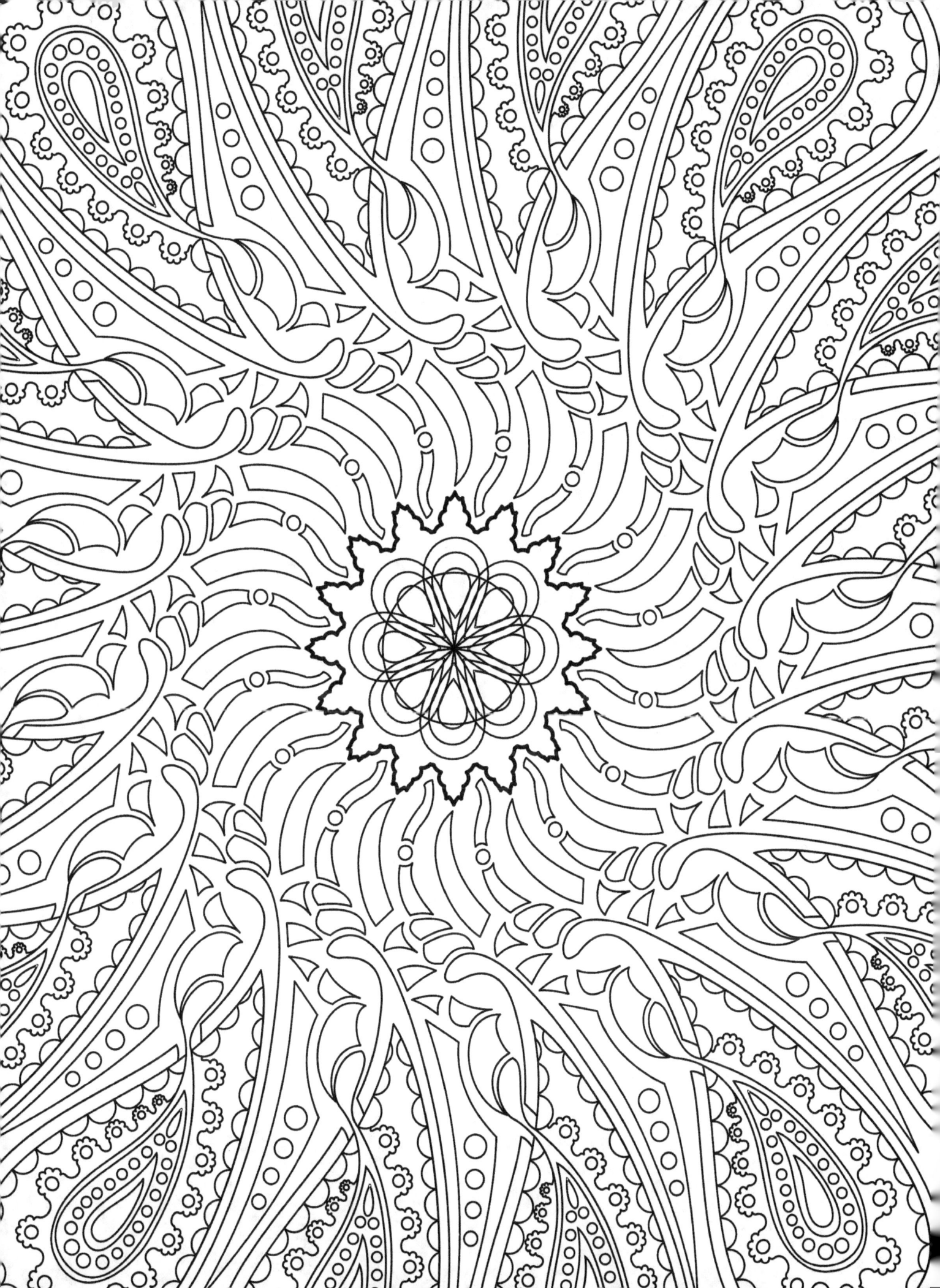

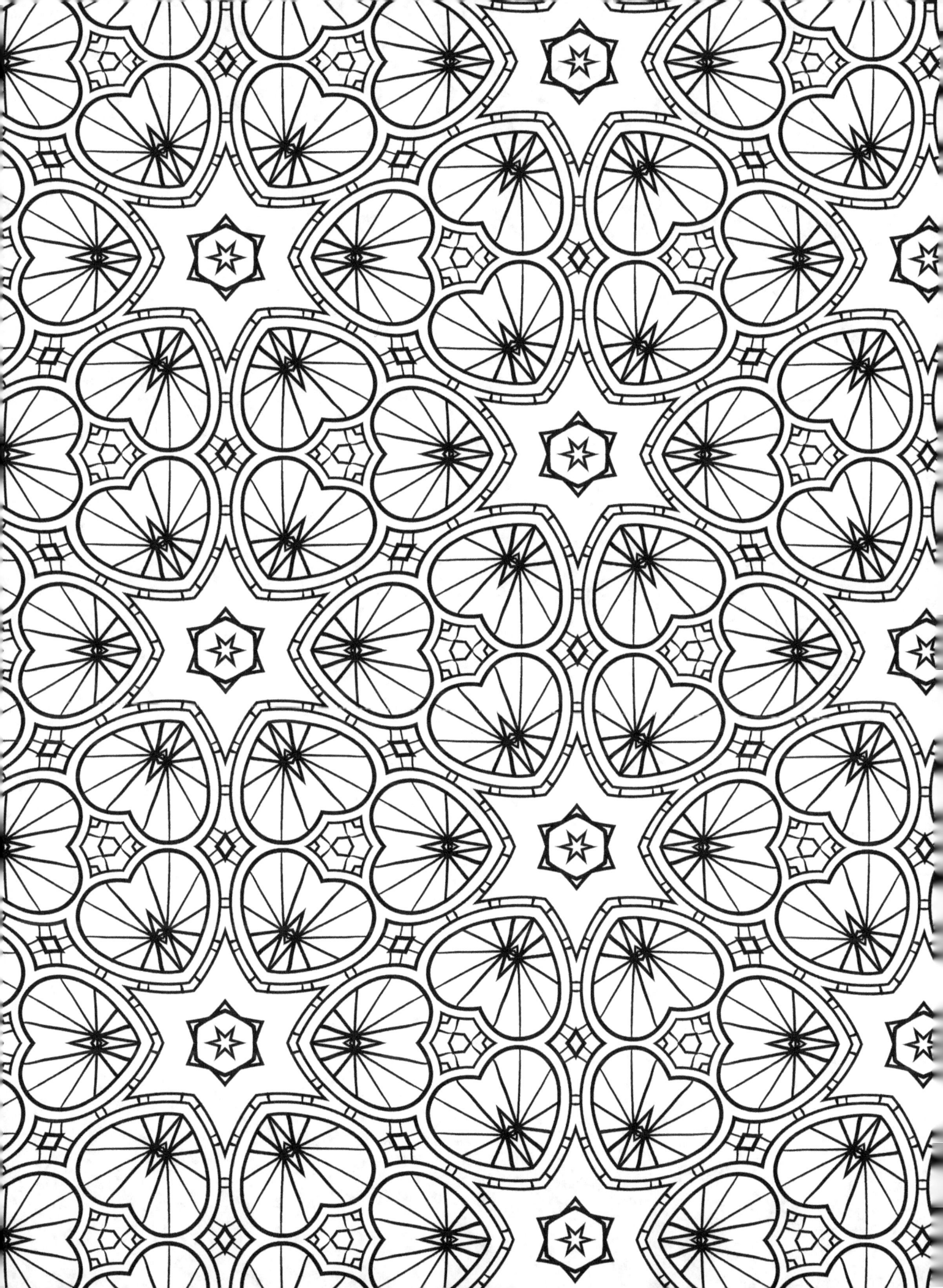

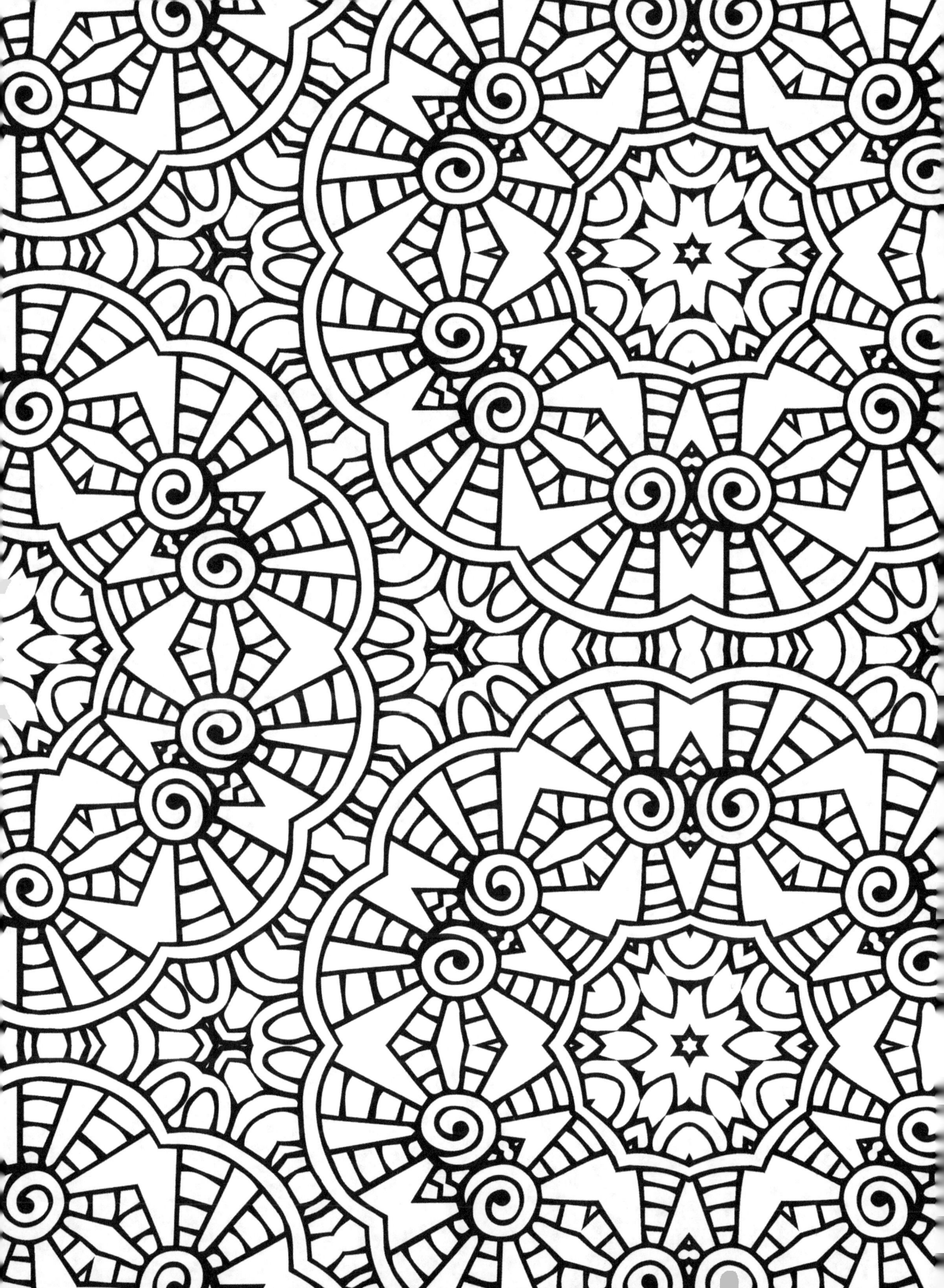

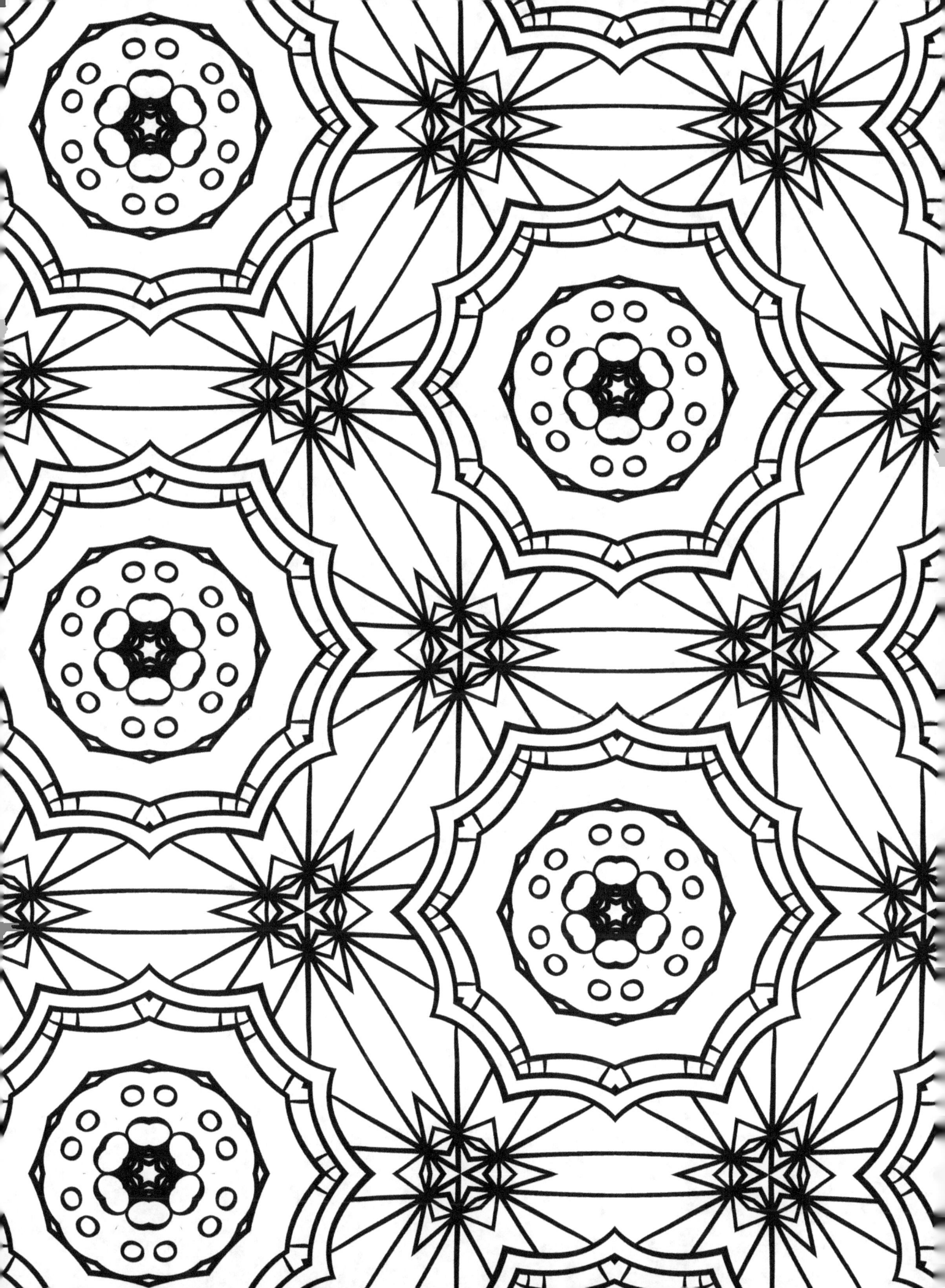

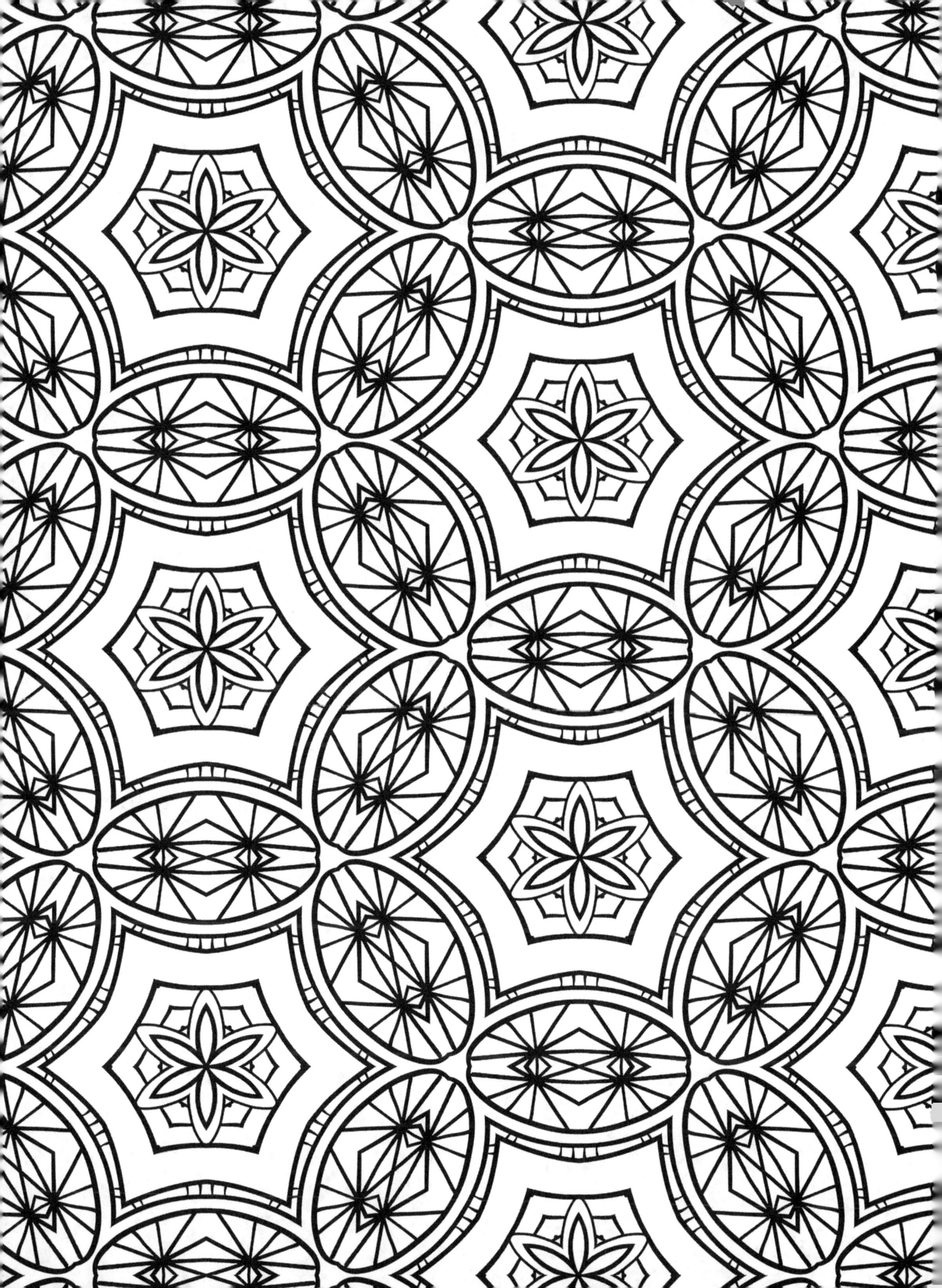

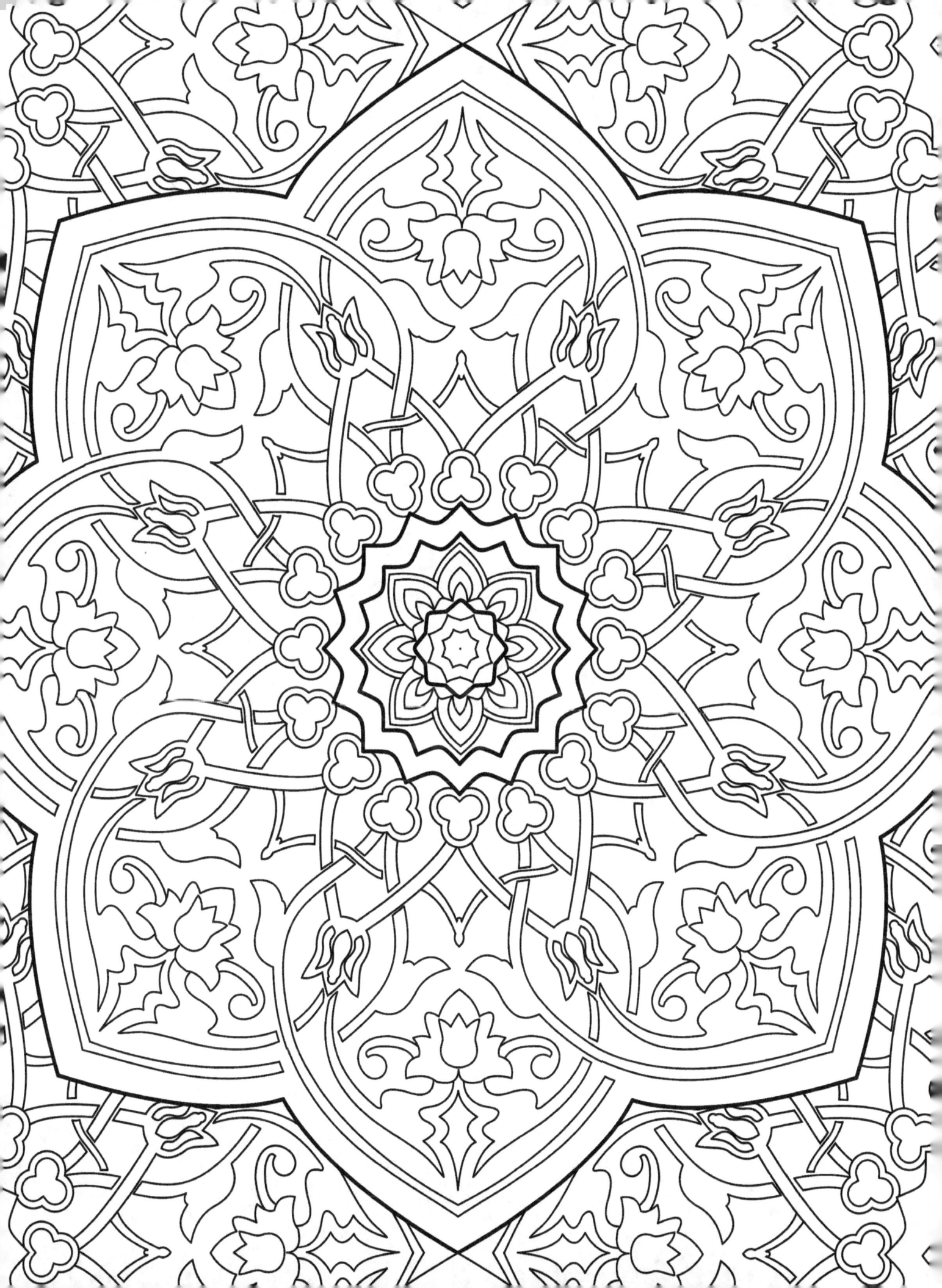

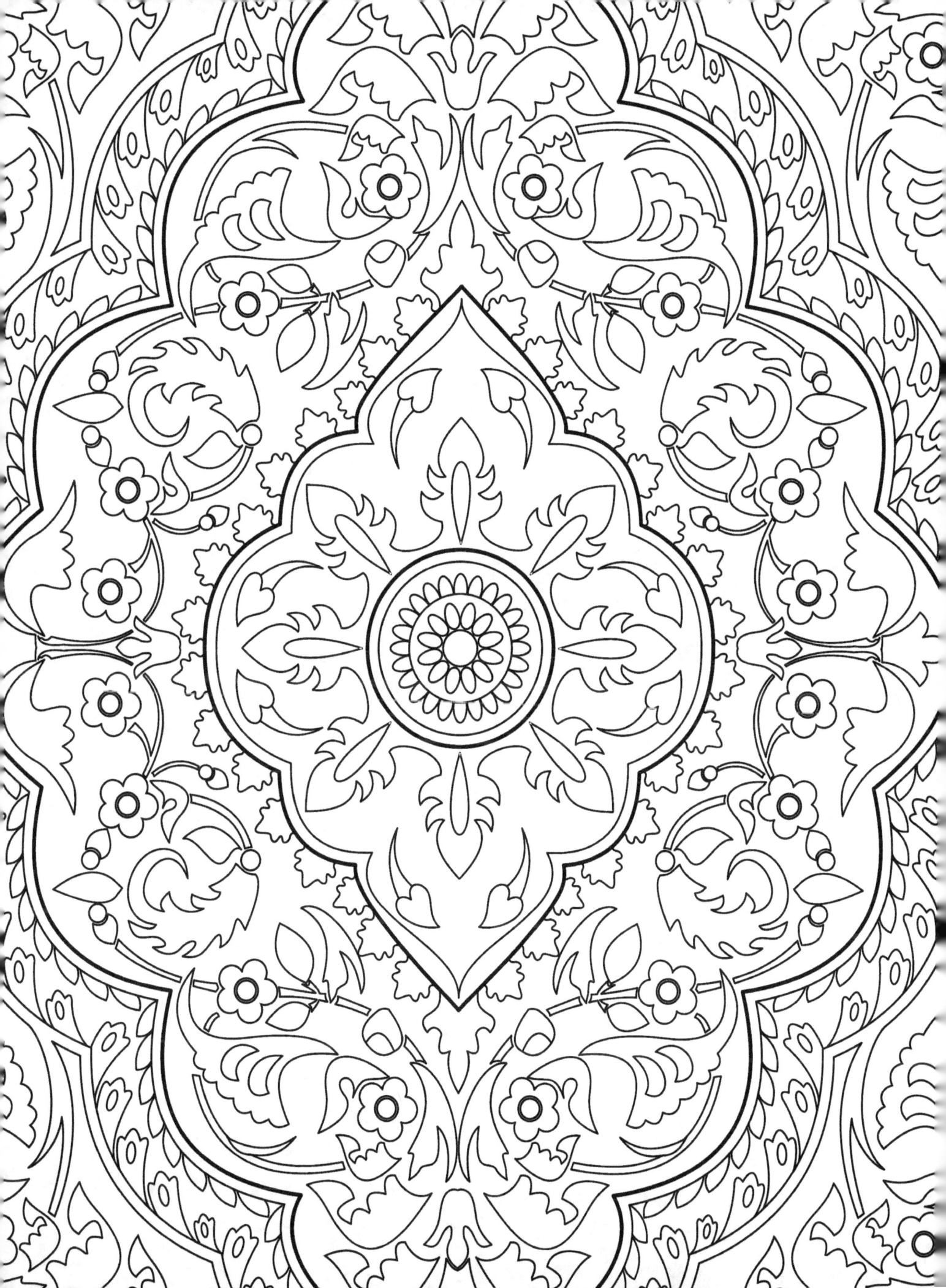

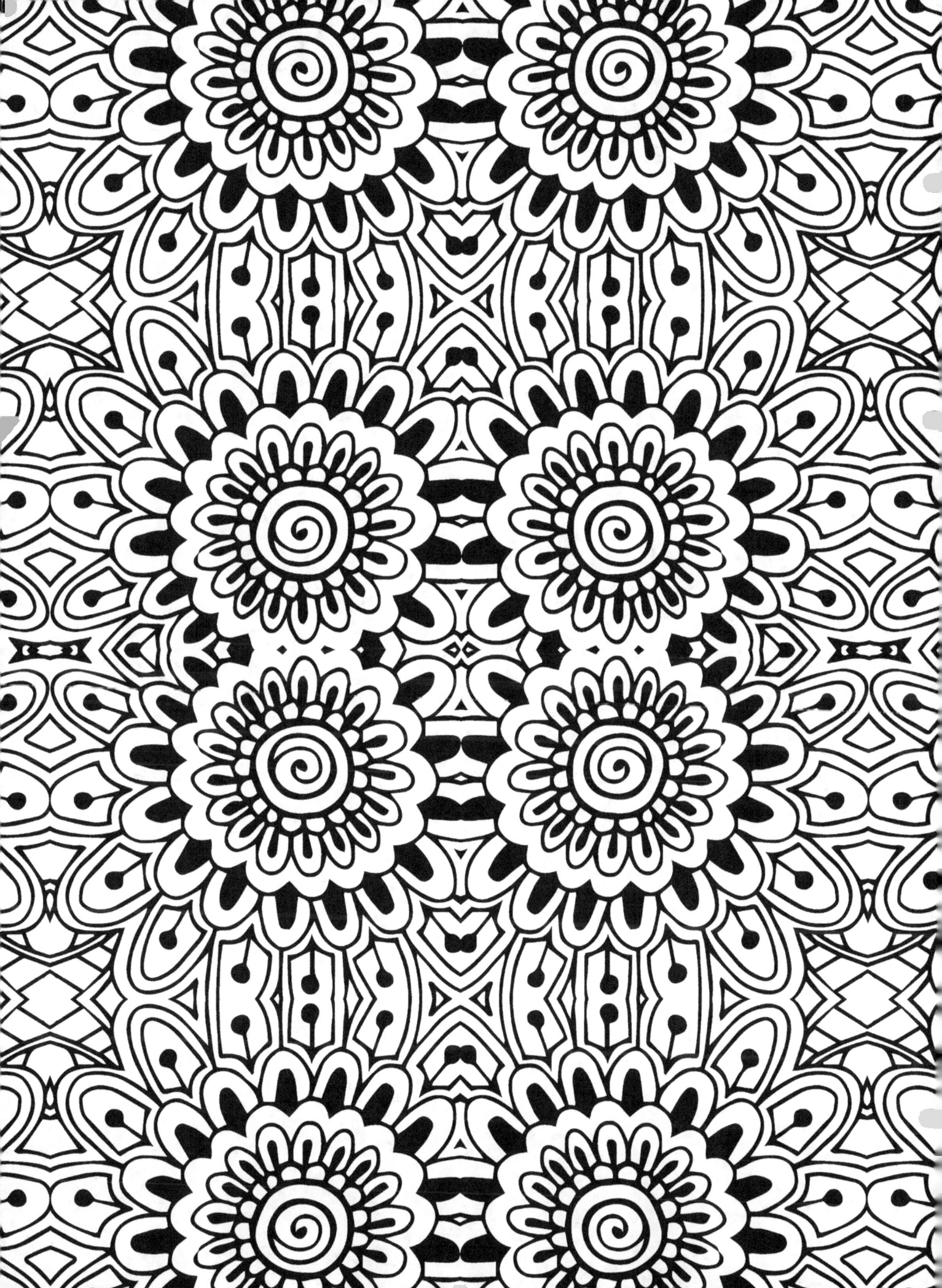

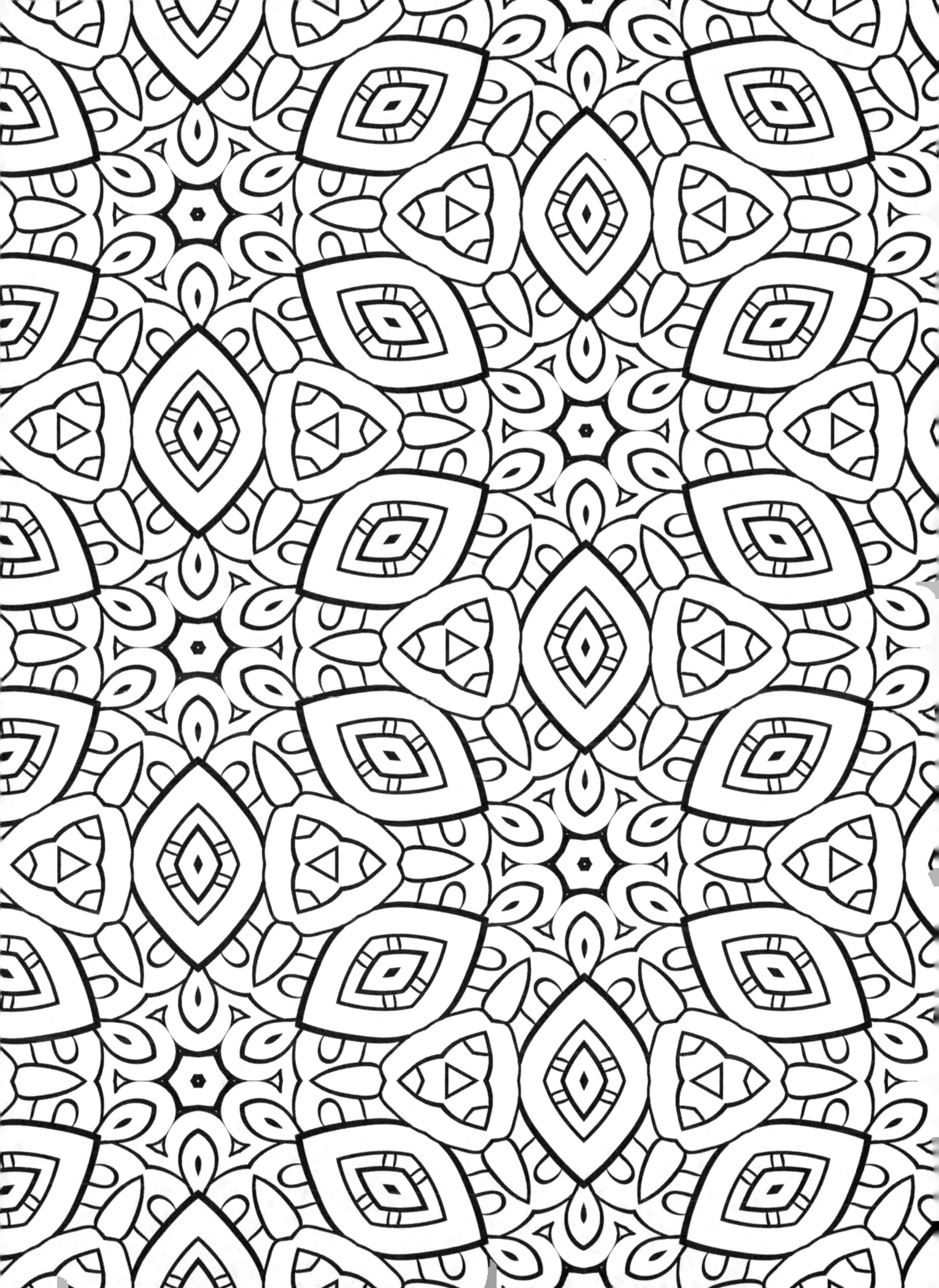

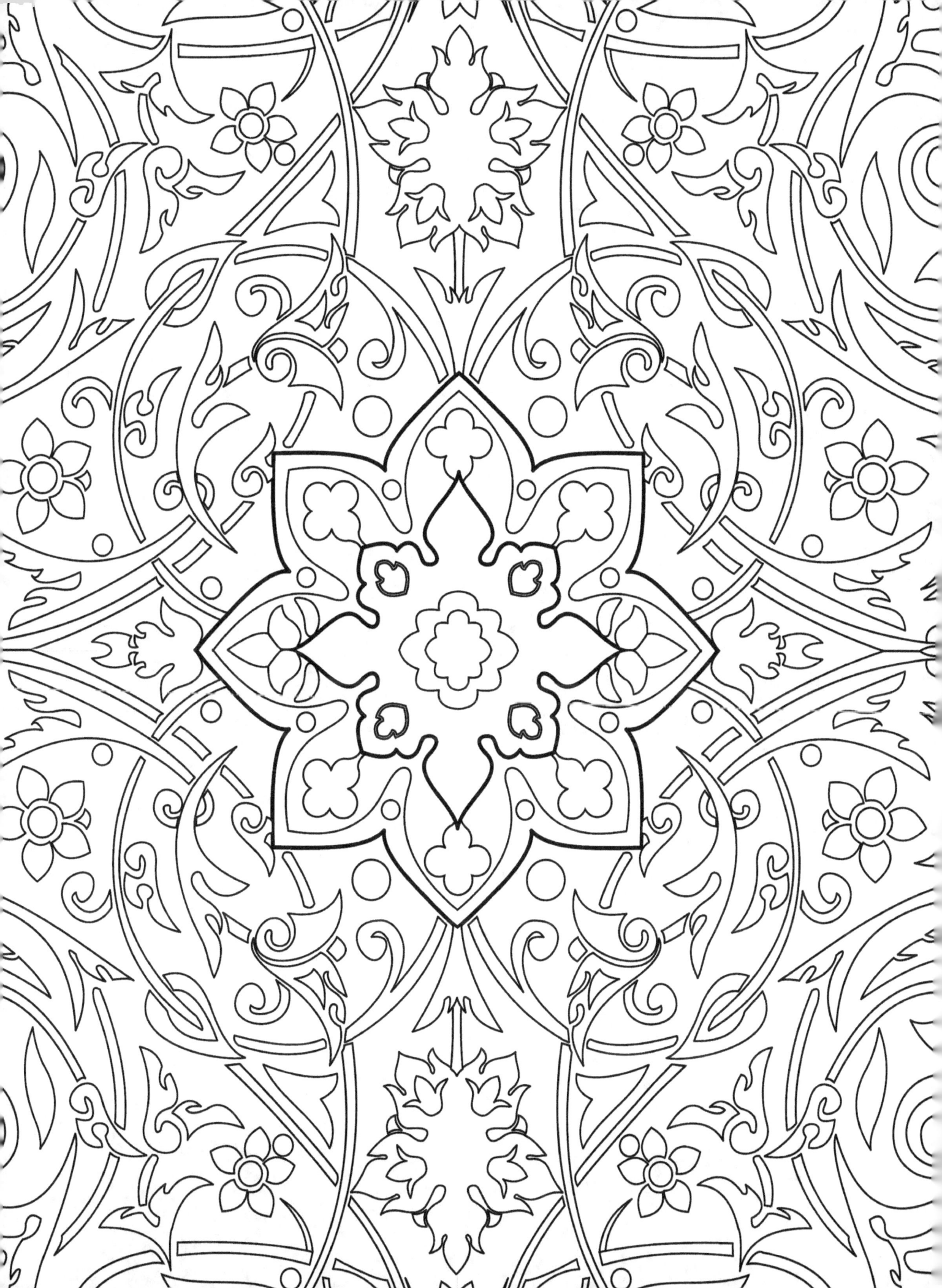

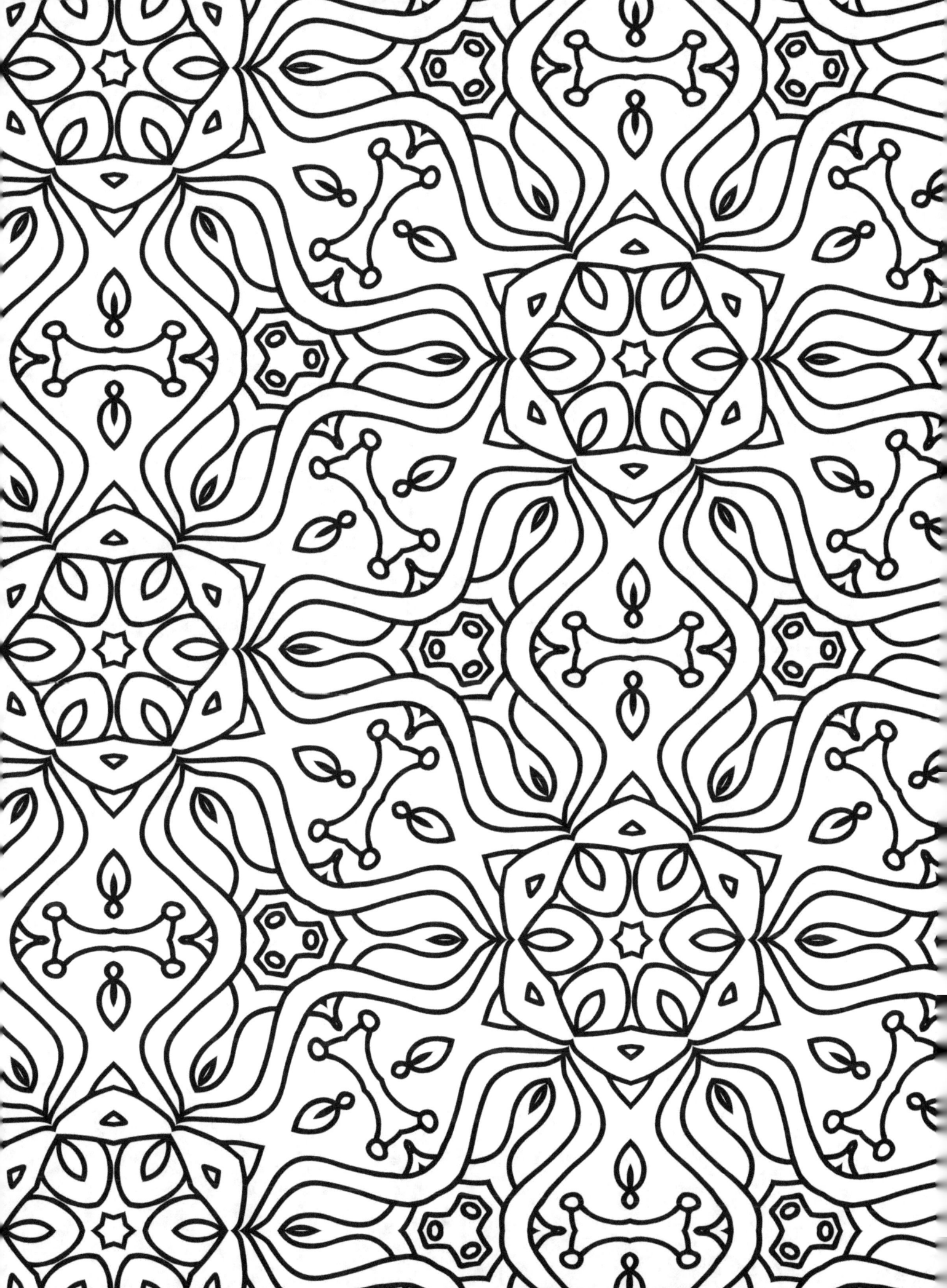

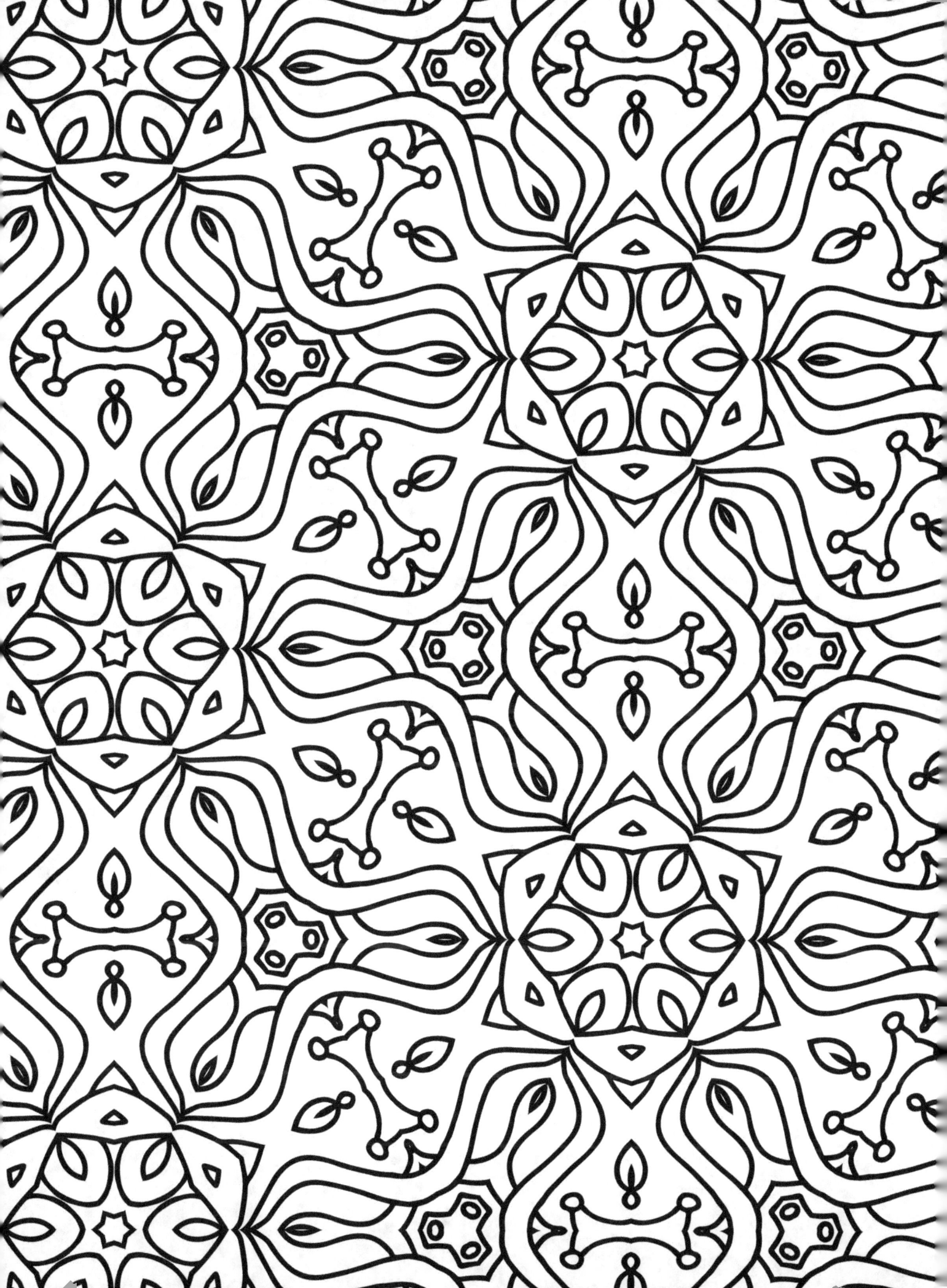

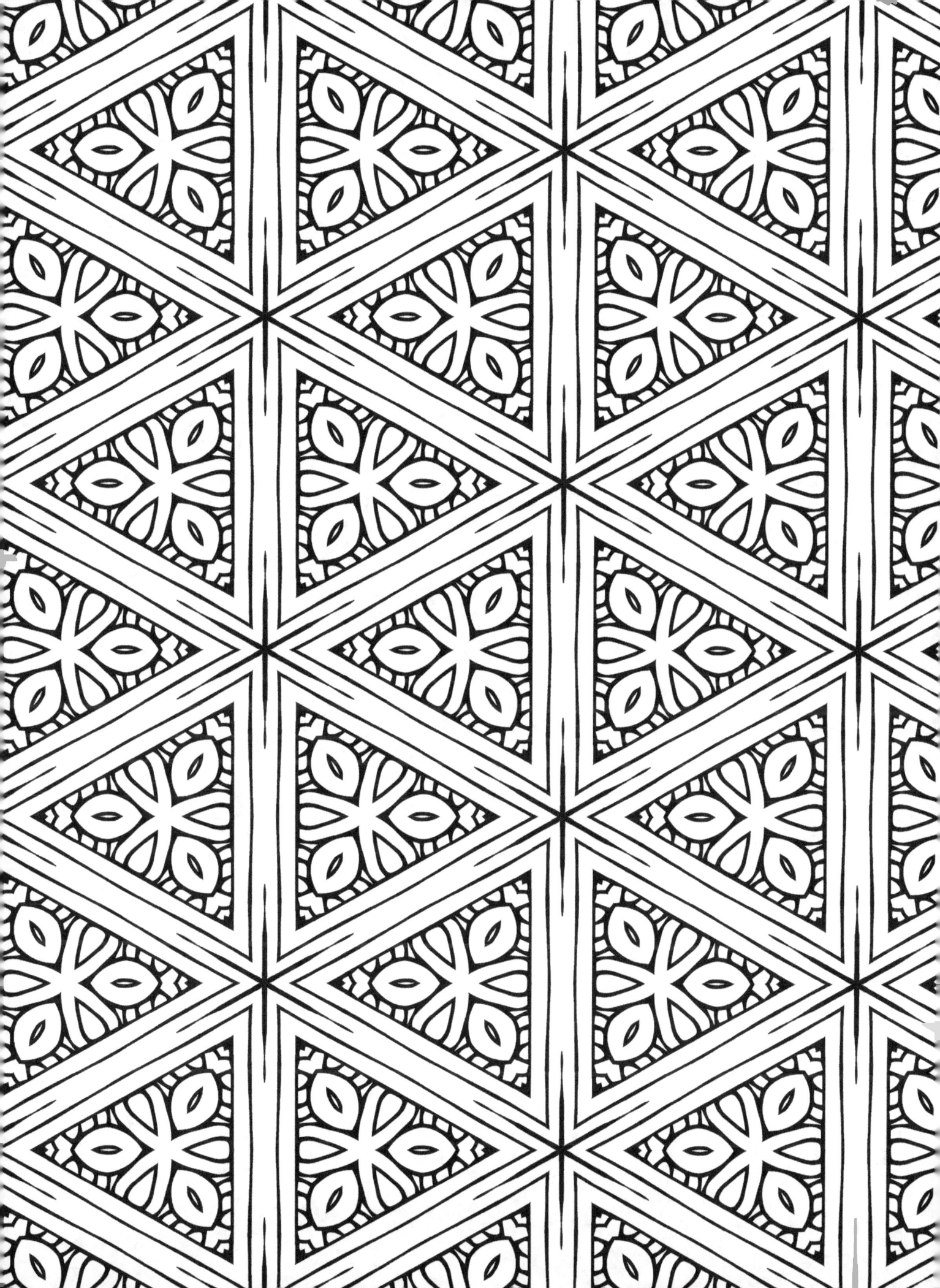

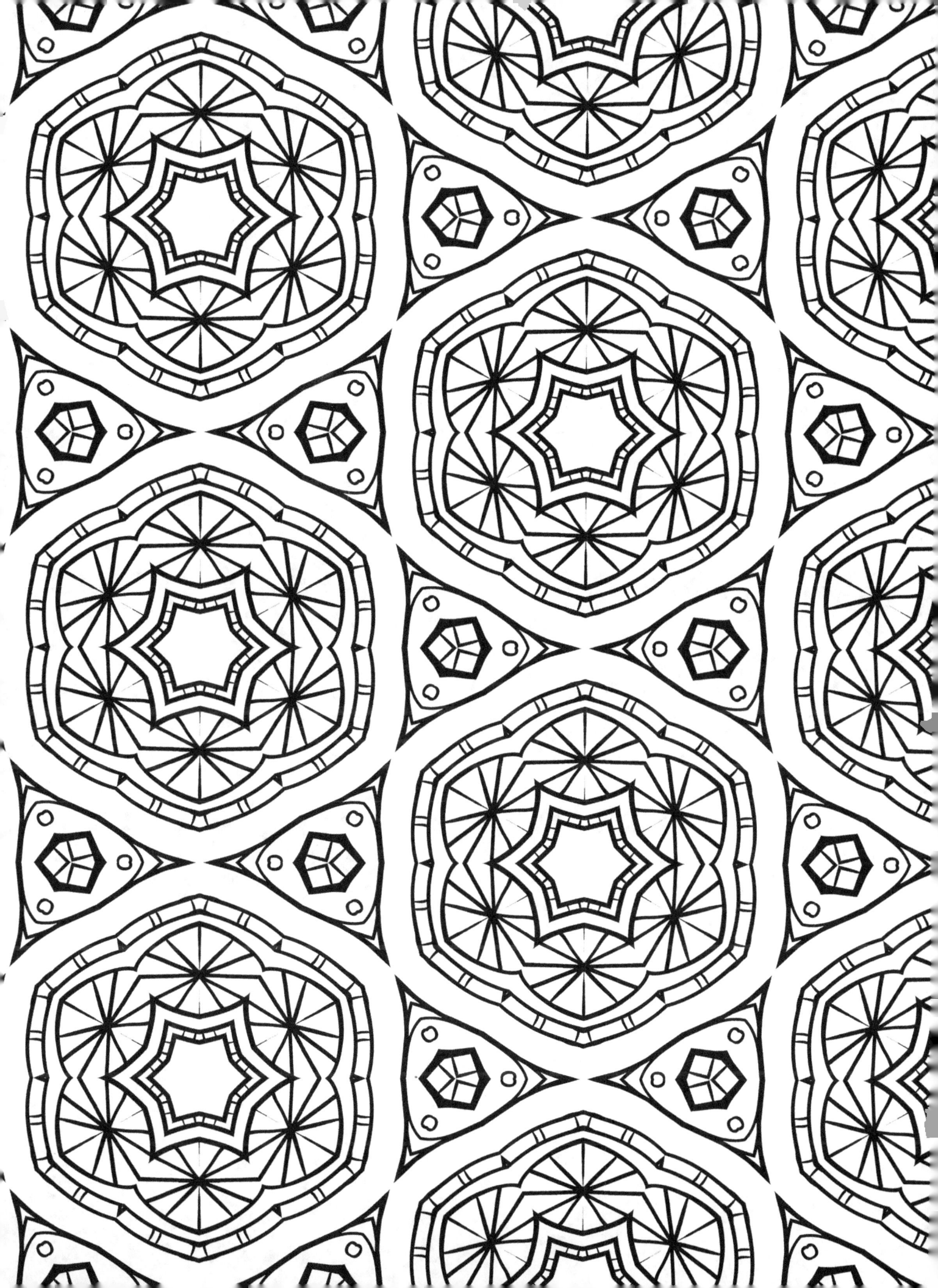

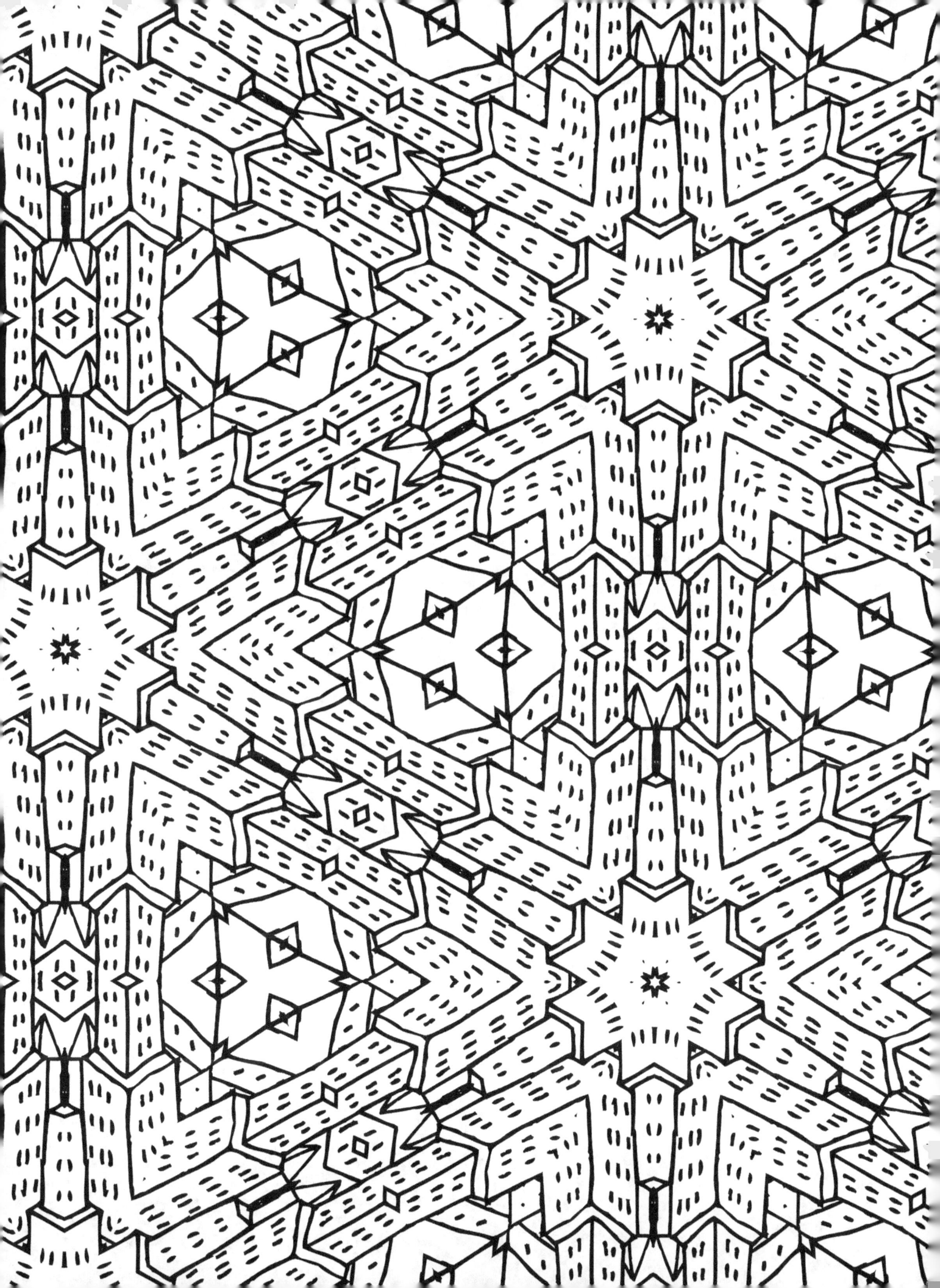

If you enjoyed colouring these designs, then move onto another book in the Progressive Patterns series of Adult Colouring Books.

We are sure you will love them!

We are amazed by the way that each of our designs looks so different when it has been coloured, so please share. We love to see your finished designs, don't be shy, head over to our Facebook page and show us what you have created.

https://www.facebook.com/progressivepatternsadultcolouringbooks

Look out for our other colouring books created by nikk nakk designs.

- Simple Styles
- Decorative Designs
- Intricate Inspirations
- Progressive Patterns Volume 1
- Progressive Patterns - A Man's World
- Progressive Patterns for Lefties
- Fairies and Flowers

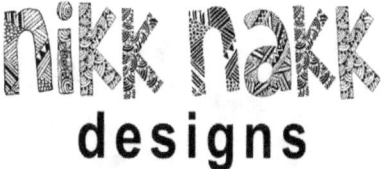